GO! GO! GO!

GO! GO! GO!

Rise, Fall & Rise Again

The Story of Cancer

Rob Atteberry

ISBN-13: 9780692758236
ISBN-10: 0692758232

Author's Note

Next to our sense of smell, it is our sense of hearing that can most naturally transport us back to a different time, place or experience. For this reason music is often linked to our memories. How often have you found yourself driving down the highway when an old song comes on the radio and you instinctively raise the volume? Do you have a specific playlist that you listen to while working out because it invigorates and motivates you? If that "one, special song" is played at a friend's wedding, do you and your spouse need only exchange a knowing glance before you both silently take the dance floor? Hearing certain songs can excite us, make us melancholy and remind us of specific times in our lives.

Since music has always been an important part of my life and an integral part of my relationship with my wife Keri, it only seemed appropriate that I use meaningful song titles to name each chapter of my story.

In this book, you will come to know both halves of my duet and our own little quartet. You'll witness firsthand "my song," with all its scores, adagio moments, ever-changing tempo, staccato sidebars and refrains, that has led me to know the greatest Maestro of this thing called "Life" as I gratefully play my encore.

In sharing my story, I've changed several names throughout this book. Any resemblance to any real person, living or dead, or any other real entity, is purely coincidental.

Dedicated to

My sons,
Max, Wes, Ben and Zac
I hope this book leads you each to live your best life.

My wife,
Keri
I love you. You are the world to me.

My dad & mom,
Max & Diane
I love you.

My Family & Friends
Your constant love and support means everything to me.

My Doctors
Thank you for your meticulous care.

Cancer Fighters & Survivors Everywhere
Never give up!

God
Thank you for each and every precious day.

Steve Ryman
Thank you for being a friend and for inspiring me to write this book.

Contents

Prologue

The exhaustion hung on me like a heavy, wet blanket I just couldn't lift away. Although I slept so much, I still never felt rested; I wondered if I would ever feel rested again. The "new me" was nothing like the person I'd been only a few months before, when my main focus had been meeting deadlines and surpassing goals to hit weekly, monthly, and quarterly numbers.

Even my reflection in the mirror bore little resemblance to the fit guy who'd once been an overachiever, competed in triathlons, and chased after his personal bests, both at work and at home. Gone were the toned biceps and defined shoulders I honed from years of swimming; the eager eyes that took on any project - big or small; and the ready grin that instantly made strangers into friends. Gone, too, were the strong arms that had held my wife and also rocked my sons; gone were the solid thighs that had characterized me as a cyclist and runner.

Who are you? I thought.

As I looked at the man in the mirror, I wondered if I'd ever again see the hard-working guy who always delivered and got the job done, no questions asked, and no matter the sacrifice. Higher sales, lower expenses, less shrink, more profits- whatever the target, I'd deliver. It was just who I was; I'd built a great career, even by working harder and longer than the next guys, and with no complaints.

*Where was **that** guy?* I wondered as I realized I missed him.

The guy in the mirror had eyes vaguely similar to mine, and yet my mind didn't want to believe they were my own. They looked dull, tired and void of their eager glimmer. It seemed so long ago that I'd dutifully left our home each morning, only to return late into the night, often after the kids had eaten dinner and taken their baths. Back then I eagerly did it all over again the next morning, after just a few hours of sleep. The pace had been nonstop, the goals never-ending, and yet, I liked it and I thought it was how things were supposed to be. I liked working; I liked my busy, goal-driven life; and I liked building a comfortable lifestyle for our family. I even liked *that other guy* who'd once met me at the mirror. I'd been proud of all he'd achieved in life.

When I'd met *him* at the mirror in days gone by, in the early morning hours and long before the sun came up, he had a familiar, eager, can-do attitude. I liked that guy's style, his character and his work ethic.

But where had he gone?

The stranger's tired eyes that stared back at me were framed by a patchy, distorted face with flakes of peeling skin in various stages of healing. I studied the haphazard palette of reds, pinks, oranges and purples that marred the stranger's sallow complexion. His ravaged face looked pained. I studied how the sickening colors framed a sunken, gray-blue pallor beneath listless, tired eyes.

The apathetic stranger looked like he'd somehow survived some terrible and life-altering event. I studied the reflection a little longer, as I turned my head to examine a new patch of raw skin that had scabbed over since the day before.

At least it's healing, I reminded myself.

While most of my hair had been gone for some time, and I really didn't miss it, the burnt, peeling, scabbed skin was definitely unattractive to say the least. If my sense of smell hadn't been diminished, I knew what

I'd smell — burnt flesh — that sickening, putrid odor of burnt skin and hair that's so distinct and repugnant, usually an unwelcome reminder of some horrific accident.

But my present condition hadn't resulted from an accident. The treatments had been ordered and efficiently scheduled. I'd gone willingly, in fact, to have them administered one by one, as the poison had rhythmically dripped into my veins, one drop at a time.

The painful burning sensation, deadened taste buds, loss of sense of smell, and itchy, flaked patches of skin had all been expected — certainly not welcomed, but expected nonetheless. My rational side reminded me that 'the guy in the mirror' was only a temporary visitor. The fatigue, pain, and unsightly discomfort were small prices to pay to still be here with Keri and the boys. I shook off the thought of the other possibilities.

Reminded of our boys, I went to join them outside, and I heard their voices become louder as I stepped out the door. Smiling to myself, I stood and watched our firstborn son, while he played in the yard with his brothers. Instantly, I was reminded that it had all been worth it, and that I'd endure it all again in a heartbeat.

Being literally cooked from the inside out, had certainly been worth it, I thought to myself, *to be here with... with...*

The tallest boy I watched was most definitely my firstborn son, and one of my greatest sources of pride and joy on this earth. I could see his name in my mind's eye, but it wouldn't come to me.

Why can't I say his name? Why can't I remember how to say the name of my own son?

My stomach felt queasy again, so I went back inside, through our home's side entrance, and into the mudroom. There was *his* jacket, and there were *his* shoes haphazardly tossed on the floor like always, and waiting for *him*... waiting for... for...

I wracked my brain, and I willed myself to put together the letters to call up his name. My mind rapidly searched its memory banks of files, again and again. I began to sweat, anxiety welled within my chest, nausea washed over me and my heart raced uncontrollably. I just couldn't make the connection, no matter how hard I tried. I knew my son's name, and yet my brain just wouldn't assimilate the letters in my head or send the word to my mouth, so I could *say* it! I slumped against the doorframe as Keri came closer.

"What is it? Rob, what's wrong?" she asked.

With tears in my eyes and a sickening feeling in the pit of my stomach, I shook my head as if to rattle loose the simplest, yet most important syllables that no father could possibly forget how to utter.

"His name," I said, with tears in my eyes. "It's like I know it, but I can't form it and say it! I can't remember how to *say* his *name*; my own son's name, Keri — the son we named after my dad!"

Keri hugged me, and held onto me, as tears fell down my face and onto my shirt.

"Max, Honey. It's Max," she said, as she rubbed my back and held me close.

1

To Be Young

By Ryan Adams

Ours had always been a fairly traditional marriage, and we had a typical household not unlike many others inside the comfortable family homes that lined our manicured street. I had married the love of my life, and I'd known Keri since she was eight and I was twelve. Although we'd known one another as kids, it wasn't until my first year out of college that we actually started to date.

Keri was 15 and I was 19 when we both had summer jobs as lifeguards at Great Oaks Country Club. My dad's job had brought our family back to Rochester. I had initially met Keri when we were on the swim team as kids. Lifeguarding was a natural fit for me, as I'd been in the pool for years by this time. Keri caught my eye, when I saw her again at the country club pool where we both worked as lifeguards; but since she was only 15, I didn't think I should ask her out — yet. Still though, working together during five-hour shifts at the pool gave us plenty of time to get to know one another. There was nothing we didn't talk about in those days.

While attending Miami University in Ohio, I moved back to Rochester in my third year of college. Both Keri and I were dating other people at

the time, and our mutual friends sometimes hung out together, which frequently put us in the same situations. I was still drawn to her infectious smile, and I quickly decided she was the nicest person I'd ever met. Before long, I couldn't stop thinking of 'cute Keri.'

Things eventually fell into place for us; and Keri and I began to see each other when she was 18. She was at Michigan State and I was working in Muskegon, but we drove to visit each other all the time. After our first date, in fact, we were basically inseparable.

Keri and I dated for five years and we became very close. One of the main things we had in common was our mutual love of music. Even in our earlier days of lifeguarding, she and I talked about and bonded over music. We spent hours making mix tapes for each other and sharing songs.

When I asked Keri to marry me, I gave her a mix-tape of songs that were special and meaningful to us. Music had always been an important part of our lives and our relationship, and it was something that would continue to be important to both of us over the years. When I gave her the mix-tape, Keri knew I'd carefully selected each song especially for her.

After a two-year engagement, Keri and I married in 2000, with all our friends and family at our wedding celebration. I was thrilled to walk into our future together, side by side with the cutest, coolest and nicest girl. Our future was bright, and we looked forward to our new life together.

Before we'd married, I'd taken a corporate job with Gechsmin, after I had previously been an area sales manager with Elder-Beerman Department Stores. In my first position with Elder-Beerman, I first oversaw three area managers and 30 to 40 associates. While I was one of the youngest managers in the company, I was good at my job, and I excelled quickly —— just like I thought I was supposed to do and just as I'd always envisioned I would do in my career.

In 1996, I took a position with the Gechsmin Corporation as a Logistics Analyst, and I steadily moved up the ranks, a year at a time. By 1999, I'd begun traveling overseas, several times a year, on business trips for a couple weeks at a time. Sometimes I went to Germany or China; and I made monthly trips to Las Vegas, Chicago, New York, LA or Florida to attend shows. It was the nature of my job, and I enjoyed the pace and the responsibility of being the face of the company. In no time, I was a Delta Platinum member, thanks to all the miles I flew.

With my career going well, I knew it was time to take another step forward in my life plan. When I married Keri in 2000, everything in my world seemed so right. I diligently steered my career, met my personal and professional goals and had married the love of my life. I was on top of the world.

Marrying Keri was another step in having my life fall into place, as I pursued our own happily ever after. Life was working out in my career and my personal life just as I'd planned. Like many men, I had a vision of the American Dream in my mind's eye; and I looked toward the nice suburban home, a beautiful wife and a houseful of children.

After our two-week Hawaiian honeymoon, I dutifully plunged into my job as a buyer for Gechsmin's Home Division, a position I'd held for about a year by this time. During our honeymoon, I kept in touch with the office and handled issues from my laptop. I'm sure Keri wasn't thrilled about it, but she knew how tenacious I'd always been about my work.

I focused on my job, determined to climb the corporate ladder and to get ahead in life, as fast as I could. The hours were many, but I had a great boss, Paula, and I was surrounded with awesome people. I thoroughly enjoyed my job, and I thrived on delivering results for a total of eight years.

The long hours and personal sacrifices had all seemed so normal to me as I rose within the company's ranks. By 2001, when I was just 29, I was named the divisional vice president in the Soft Home division. I'll admit I loved what I did. I'll even go so far as to say it exhilarated and energized me to oversee a sales volume of more than $2 billion and a staff of 12, which included six buyers. Responsible for the company's Bedding, Bath, Window, Kitchen Textiles and Floor categories, I developed the Thalia brand in Soft Home that focused heavily on the Hispanic demographic. As a divisional VP, I expanded our Martha Stewart brand and introduced new products. I also reintroduced the line's 3-, 4- and 5-star bed and bath products.

While I worked hard to get ahead for Keri and myself, we were blessed with our first child, a son. Max was born in 2002 and was instantly the light of our lives. Our newly expanded young family lived in a condo in Rochester. With my dad's help, we'd worked hard together for many months to renovate the condo; and it was perfect for us at the time.

For the first three months after Max's birth, Keri continued her work as a first grade teacher. We were fortunate to have our parents help us care for little Max, but Keri and I both made the decision that she should stay home with our new son.

Life couldn't have been better, from where I stood. I had a beautiful wife, a precious new son and a great career. There was a lot happening in our lives at the time, and I enjoyed the pulse and pace of it all. It felt like the puzzle pieces were all falling into place, and as if Keri and I were on our way to creating the perfect American Dream.

Before long, I was promoted to divisional vice president of Soft Home and Hard Home with Gechsmin. Our son was walking, talking and discovering his new world, and I was working hard to broaden my own horizons

in order to give my family the life they deserved. It felt good to be our family's provider and it was a role I relished.

By 2003, I was managing both the Soft and Hard Home teams, and was responsible for direct reports of buying and indirect reports of finance, advertising and store operations. With 10 buying teams, each comprised of 20 or more team members, including two merchandising managers, I was responsible for a $3 billion segment of the company. Happily ensconced in my fast-paced corporate career, I also managed the $1.2 billion Martha Stewart Home brand for the company, with responsibilities that included brand development, marketing efforts and in-store presentations, among countless other things.

When handled correctly, retail means revenues, and revenues mean dollars for everyone in the company. It was the perfect cause-and-effect example of how hard work and dedication pay off. It made sense, and it worked well with plans for my family's lifestyle and my own career path. I did my job, and I did it well. I continued to rise within the corporate ranks at a young age. Everything was working out according to my plan, and I had the world by the tail, as far as I was concerned. My future looked bright and hopeful from where I stood in those early days. Only the sky seemed to be the limit, and I was determined to keep growing and improving as I built my career.

In less than a year as a divisional vice president, Gechsmin promoted me again, this time to vice president/GMM of Home and Home Electronics. As the title and the salary grew, so too did the responsibilities and the workload. I was managing a $5 billion sales volume and overseeing 18 buying teams with over 40 team members and three divisional merchandise managers. I thrived in a high-pressure atmosphere, and I really enjoyed that my progress was measurable and marked, even in just one year, as I increased our gross margin and reduced inventory cost dollars by

20 percent. Again, there was a direct effect that reflected my efforts, and I liked being in control of our progress and contributing to the company's growth.

I was prepared to put in the work and the time to keep moving ahead. The corporate ladder held such promise, and I liked the idea that I was in control of my destiny and that life was working out just as it should.

2

Begin the Begin

By REM

While my corporate responsibilities increased, so had my results, and Gechsmin wasn't the only corporation to notice. After just a year in my vice president role with Gechsmin, I was recruited by another hypermarket giant. Founded in 1934 as a supermarket, but later credited with pioneering the supercenter concept in 1962, Tendlart was a major player in the retail world. When they recruited me, Tendlart was on its way to becoming one of America's largest private companies and one of North America's top food retailers. The work ethic of Tendlart's founder, Hendrik Tendlart, a Dutch immigrant, mirrored my own.

I'd resigned from Gechsmin on good terms and with notice, and I had eagerly accepted Tendlart's offer to be a vice president. The only negative thing about the job was that it required us to leave our extended family and move to Grand Rapids. We found a lot in a beautiful neighborhood and began the process of building a house. I moved into an apartment near work, while Keri and Max stayed behind for eight months. Keri and I were a team, and we each did what we had to do to make things work for our family.

In my position with Tendlart, I was responsible for merchandising strategy and personnel development for the Do It Yourself, Automotive, Garden, Pets and Electronics/Media teams. I jumped into my role with enthusiasm and worked harder than ever, with my eye on the prize: to make a great life for our family.

Since I'd known at the time that Gechsmin would be moving their headquarters and we didn't want to leave our Michigan family, Keri and I felt like the Tendlart offer had come at a good time. Keri did her part and took care of Max and our home, while I concentrated on my new role with Tendlart.

We moved to Ada, a suburb outside of Grand Rapids, when Max was two-and-a-half years old. Things seemed nearly perfect! We were still close enough to everyone that Keri and I could see our families and friends on the weekends; and Keri stayed home and took care of Max. It felt like we were building our American Dream, and I liked the idea that I was providing an ideal life for my family, as I'd always wanted to do.

My twelve-hour workdays just became the norm for Keri and me. She never complained about having to shoulder the bulk of the parenting responsibilities, and we each fell into our traditional roles of provider and caretaker. I took care of our finances and stability and handled the big picture, while Keri managed 'home and hearth' and took care of the day-to-day details for our family. It was an exhilarating time, and I basked in my responsibilities.

Our families and friends have always been important to Keri and me, and we continued to see them every week, even after we'd moved to Grand Rapids. We wanted Max to grow up surrounded by family and good influences. It was all part of our traditional expectations and our own upbringings.

Many days — and nights — were spent focused on my job with Tendlart. I was responsible for 14 buying teams of over 60 team members,

which included three merchandise managers. It exhilarated me to manage over $1.1 billion in sales, and to work with others to better their own careers, as I furthered mine. My employees, my boss, my company and my family all relied on me for results, and that was perfectly fine with me. In my mind, I was doing what was expected of me and what was required to secure a good life. I'd never shied away from hard work, and I continued to push and push toward bigger, higher goals. I wasn't certain where my efforts would ultimately lead, but I was prepared to go the distance, no matter what.

Keri and I were both thrilled when we learned she was pregnant with our second child, Wes. We were at a good place in our lives, and it was a good time to add to our family. In 2006, Wes joined our family, and Keri and I were thrilled that Max, three-and-a-half by the time, had a little brother.

With a newborn and an active toddler, Keri definitely had her hands full at home. We made a great team, although both of us were tired each night by the time we dropped into bed. Since she knew I had to be at work early in the morning, Keri always got up with Wes for his nighttime feedings and diaper changes. She was a natural mother and she made it look easy. Having her at home with my boys made it easy for me to go to work and focus on my corporate responsibilities. I knew I was a lucky man though, and for so many reasons.

About a year after our second son was born, Tendlart asked me to take over in 2007 as vice president of Home and Electronics & Media. I was up for the challenge, and I plunged in headfirst to my new position, responsible for merchandising strategies and personnel development of the Home areas.

With 16 teams of 70 people and three merchandise managers, I was responsible for $1 billion in volume. While some people might have considered this a pressure position, I loved it. Within three years, I'd established strategic principles for pricing, marketing, store presentation, brands and merchandise assortment across all business groups in my division. By 2010, the results of my efforts were once again measurable in increased year-over-year sales figures and a gain in market share that showed Tendlart had outpaced other retailers in the electronics industry for three years in a row.

While Keri managed our family and our home life, I managed the development and negotiation of multiple private label programs. As Keri handled the needs of our boys, I handled my employees and my corporate responsibilities. She and I were a team, each managing our own parts of the equation that would ultimately create the life we'd envisioned for our family.

With Max in Kindergarten and Wes only a year old, we learned our family would be expanding again. Keri had her first ultrasound halfway through her pregnancy, at 20 weeks; and of course I was with her.

The ultrasound technician applied the sticky gel to Keri's abdomen and then moved her probe across Keri's skin as she looked at the screen. Her eyes got bigger, and Keri and I looked at each other.

"What is it?" I asked. "Everything okay with the baby?"

"Have you had a previous ultrasound?" asked the technician.

We hadn't had one before that day, and Keri and I looked at each other with worried expressions, afraid something might be wrong with the baby.

"Well, you're having *twins*!" the technician hesitated.

"Ummm... What?" Keri asked.

Keri and I both took deep breaths and tried to absorb what we'd just heard. We were overwhelmed, extremely surprised, and so, so happy. Of course, they were both boys.

I think Keri was still numb with shock, as the technician wiped off the sticky gel and helped her to sit up again. She and I didn't say much as we walked out of the obstetrician's office.

"Hungry?" I asked as we walked to our car.

"Of course. Let's get some pizza. Apparently, I'm eating for three!"

A few minutes later, Keri and I sat across from each other at a pizzeria. She and I just stared at each other as our new reality sunk in. It was a lot to absorb.

"Twins," she said.

"Yeah. Wow. At least we know how to raise boys already."

"What. Are. We. Gonna. Do?" Keri said.

Then we both burst out laughing, and it was as if we both knew we'd be just fine.

"It's twins!" we happily told our family and friends. "Both boys!"

Everyone's eyes got big when we told them we had not one, but *two* more boys on the way.

"Are you guys trying to start your own basketball team?" friends joked.

Keri and I were thrilled though, and we'd certainly had plenty of practice with boys by this time. Even throughout her pregnancy with the twins, Keri still managed our household and our two small boys. She was awesome, and I appreciated how she kept everything together, so I could focus on my work.

By the time in 2008 when Ben and Zac came along, Keri had really learned to multi-task. While she made it all seem so easy, it would be some time before I realized the impact it was having on her.

3

I'm Ready

By Twin Shadow

While I put in 80 to 100 hours a week at work, Keri held down the fort at home. We had a wonderful sitter, Abby, to help Keri with the boys' evening routines, and give her a slight break; although taking care of four boys under the age of five was still a lot. Abby was the cousin of a neighbor and a college student when she began to help with the boys. She was an amazing help and quickly became part of our family.

As I'd leave for work in the mornings, Keri would ask, "So, do you think we'll see you before 8 p.m. tonight? Maybe we can all eat dinner together."

"I'll try, but I just never know how the day will play out," I'd answer as I kissed her goodbye.

Whenever we had all the kids in the car, on the way to dinner or to visit family, I'd conditioned the boys to "keep quiet while Dad's on a business call." My workdays didn't really end once I'd left the office. Deadlines, figures and issues still swirled around my head, as if part of my makeup.

It was Abby who helped Keri with dinner and bath time for the boys. I missed out on feedings, bath time, story time, and rocking the boys to sleep, as I dutifully did what I thought I was supposed to do in my role as

a dad and a husband. It would be years later until I learned that Keri had dressed newborn Max in cute little outfits every day at 5 p.m., in hopes that Daddy would be home to see him.

But Keri never complained. She was my support system and the reason I was able to rise in the ranks as a successful executive. Looking back, I think we each expected things to slow down and normalize in time. But the clock was ticking and the calendar pages kept flipping as my boys grew up. As well as I controlled aspects of my professional world I still had no control over how quickly time passed.

When the boys started playing soccer and swimming, Keri drove them to their practices. I made it to their games and meets, but I was *that dad* who was always dressed in business clothes, and with a cell phone to his ear, as I paced on the sidelines.

"Dad! Dad! Did you see it, Dad?" they'd ask excitedly after a game. "Did you see me score?"

"Yeah, Buddy! That was awesome!" I'd say, as I covered the mouthpiece of the phone that was still glued to my ear.

Even if I had to travel in late December, I always made it home for Christmas. But as Keri busily cooked dinner in the kitchen, I could often be found on my cell phone, cloistered away in my home office and dealing with work-related issues. Again, I felt like I was doing what I had to do, and what was expected of me.

I loved my boys more than anything, and would do anything in the world for them, but it was Keri who at times insisted I give the boys their baths or help them with their reading. It wasn't that she wanted me to do it, but rather that she wanted to give me the experience of doing it with our sons, before the opportunity was lost.

My dad had been the same too. He'd always been the main breadwinner and the parent who went out and worked while Mom raised the kids at

home. It seemed to me that if I worked and brought in a huge salary for my family, that I was meeting expectations and fulfilling my role in life. But Keri was sort of a single parent at times. As much as I wanted the boys to call for me, it was *Mommy* who they called out for if they had a nightmare or a scraped knee, and *whom* the boys wanted to put a Band-Aid on their injuries. It's what they'd known, while Daddy was away at the office or off on a business trip.

While I thought I was handling my role of the traditional father as was expected, I'd later learn that Keri wasn't as thrilled. She had grown envious of some of the other women in our neighborhood whose husbands arrived home by 5:30 like clockwork every evening, while her husband was still at the office.

My boys were growing up though, and becoming mannerly, articulate and smart. Yet it was Mom who had swaddled them, taught them, soothed them and guided them in their early years. It was Mom who helped with homework, celebrated lost teeth, refereed squabbles, soothed hurt feelings and dealt with the allergies that afflicted all of our boys.

While Keri handled the parenting at home, I was ensconced in my corporate world with Tendlart, and many changes that were going on within the 80-year-old company. Unlike Gechsmin with its more than 3,000 stores and corporate atmosphere, Tendlart had grown to 160 stores, one at a time, by the time I came onboard. Tendlart didn't seem to have the same infrastructure I'd grown accustomed to at Gechsmin. That was what I brought to Tendlart in the Home & Hard Lines areas. My mission was to make Electronics the best in the area, and anchor it with a solid Photo

Processing section. I understood the company's strengths and weaknesses, and I knew what the company needed from me and what I could contribute.

I had a great counterpart in Ruth, and although my boss was nice enough to me, he had a reputation for not being nice to all the other employees. He was an intense sort of guy with a passion for Excel spreadsheets, and he loved his PowerPoint presentations. He expected all his people to be prepared for the company's Monday morning meetings and to show up armed with their individual 20-page reports, even if the reports had consumed their entire weekends. It was just how he was, and it was known throughout the company that he expected everyone to fall into step with him, no questions asked, no excuses accepted. Even if I didn't agree with his management strategy or his tactics, I was a company guy, so I delivered at all costs, even throughout the constant stress.

My boss also had a reputation for being a talker, and for never letting others get a word in edgewise. He also loved his graphs, charts and reports, and he was a paperwork guy who insisted on having things done his way. I imagined his entire life was charted on the spreadsheets he loved so much. He was three years older than I was and I sometimes saw him at the gym. He and I worked out together a few times.

Our president called me one day and said, "Look Rob, I know the guy is tough."

The guy was one of those managers who presumed his job was to identify all the negatives, find fault and call attention to problems. If there weren't any, he'd create some. I spent a lot of my time dealing with his idiosyncrasies and time-wasting requirements.

Things had become very tenuous at work when my boss came onboard and they only became worse still in time. I knew he didn't particularly like me, but his boss, the company president, liked me and we were in fact, friends.

By this time, I'd begun to feel some stress and it had begun to affect my sleep too. Coupled with a bothersome sinus irritation, I spent most nights tossing and turning and trying to get comfortable in a position that allowed me breathe. Each night, as soon as I'd lie down, I noticed my sinuses felt congested, and predictably, the 'battle for sleep' began. When the alarm went off each morning, I dragged myself from our bed and into the shower, so I could wake-up and start the cycle all over again.

I felt tired most of the time, but since I hadn't been sleeping well, I attributed it to that fact. I'd also begun to get frequent nosebleeds that came on quickly, with no warning; and lasted quite a while.

One night, while at the movies with Keri, I suddenly got a nosebleed. While she ran to get some napkins for me, I wondered why the nosebleeds seemed to be happening more and more often. Keri and I had presumed it must be the result of whatever sinus condition afflicted me. I stopped the bleeding and went on with life as usual.

After eight years with Tendlart, and no telling how much precious family time and the boys' "firsts" forever lost, our company president called me into his office one day. What happened next came as a shock. For the first time in my life, I was unceremoniously let go from my job.

That very afternoon, I phoned Bruce, the president of Hydeswort Companies whom I'd known from Gechsmin.

"Sure! Come on over and we can walk the place and talk about a possible VP position for you," Bruce said.

A week later, I met with him in Detroit and was hired. Relationships, networking and my own reputation had paid off for me.

4

Something's Wrong

By Sloan

I was eager to jump into my new job with Hydeswort Companies, America's leading manufacturer and marketer of outdoor cushions, furniture and décor. I was based out of Hydeswort's corporate office in Detroit in my new position as Vice President of New Business Development. The logistics meant that Keri and the boys lived in Grand Rapids to finish out the school year, while I lived with my parents in Detroit. It wasn't an ideal situation, but once again, Keri and I worked as team, each of us handling our specific responsibilities to make things work.

As always, I plunged headfirst into my new role, intently focused on getting results and making a name for myself with Hydeswort. I immediately established a New Business Team, implemented a new product process to be used across the company for future business ideas and developed and implemented new market strategies for the company. With nearly two decades of experience in retail management and executive administration, I was in my element and energized by the prospects of my future with the company.

While I was busy with my corporate life, working twelve hours a day and making buying trips to China, Keri continued to take care of our four boys at home in Grand Rapids while we built our new home in Clarkston. I was approaching my 40th birthday, and it felt like I had the perfect life on all fronts.

The only thing that hindered me in the slightest was a nagging sinus infection that had started well over a year earlier, and had followed me from Tendlart to Hydeswort. I'd taken all the usual over-the-counter sinus medications, and I even saw a doctor who prescribed some antibiotics, but nothing seemed to work to lessen the sinus symptoms.

I felt even worse at nighttime, had trouble breathing and couldn't sleep well. When I'd competed in a triathlon my sinus infection had made it hard to breathe. I'd completed many triathlons, so I knew it was unusual for me to feel that way.

"I wonder when this infection will clear up," I said to Keri one night after I'd come home late from work. "I've never had a cold or sinus problem that hung on for so long."

"Well, I bought you a new hypoallergenic allergy pillow today," she said. "I thought maybe you have allergies, instead of a sinus infection. It's worth a try."

But even the new allergy pillow made no difference. I still couldn't sleep and as a result, I didn't feel rested during the workday. The longer this went on, the worse I felt. I was approaching forty though, so I assumed I was just getting a little older, so perhaps I needed to get more exercise in order to improve my sleep quality. I was certain that whatever afflicted me had a simple explanation. I just hoped I'd feel better for my upcoming birthday celebration that was coming up in a few months.

We went through the holidays of 2011, enjoyed a great Christmas with our boys and our families, and we looked toward the promise of the New Year. I felt tired, but I figured my non-stop work life was just catching up with me, and that I simply needed some rest. That nagging sinus infection had never gone away, so I still wasn't sleeping well at night.

Just six days into 2012, I'd had enough of feeling lousy and Keri took me to the ER. The doctor examined me, told me that something had been going around, and prescribed more antibiotics with instructions to "take all the medication, drink plenty of fluids and use a humidifier at night" when I slept.

As the seasons changed and we went into springtime, I still had gotten no relief, and the doctors continued to diagnose *acute rhinitis* and *acute maxillary sinusitis*. The doctors prescribed still more antibiotics, steroids, for the inflammation, and nasal inhalers.

"Drink plenty of water," the doctors reminded me, "And get lots of rest."

Keri had made all the arrangements for my 40th birthday. Somehow, between juggling all her responsibilities of mothering four boys on her own, while we were living apart, she put together an incredible celebration.

Family and friends have always been so important to me, with my love for music following close behind. Even though I didn't feel well, I was determined to enjoy my birthday surrounded by the people who meant the most to me.

When Saturday night came, a dozen couples, made up of our closest friends and family, joined us in downtown Detroit. Keri had set-up everything in advance and had reserved hotel rooms at a casino. With friends,

family and music, it was sure to be the perfect birthday. Keri reserved a VIP area at a nightclub, but she'd expected we'd all gamble first at the casino, and then go to the nightclub as a secondary option. As it turned out, our fun, eclectic group danced the night away in the nightclub till 3 a.m.

My sister Cindy even made my birthday cake, shaped like an old-style Atari console- something that only people of "my generation" would recognize. It felt so good to turn 40 surrounded by the people I loved. Life was good, and the future seemed even brighter when I shut my eyes and held my wife after we'd partied the night away. It felt like I had it all. Life was coming together just as I'd wanted.

Life looked terrific from where I stood – except for that nagging sinus condition that I just couldn't shake. I finally went to my childhood doctor and he decided to look further into my sinus issue. I'd had a CT scan done a week before my party, and so Keri and I assumed we'd soon have some answers. I figured my doctor would simply change my medication and that I'd soon be well.

Living in two different households was far from ideal – for any of us – but we knew it was just a temporary arrangement since the boys needed to complete the school year in Grand Rapids. Keri and I didn't like it, but we still made it work from different sides of the state.

Just days before I'd turned 40, I went on a buying trip to China. Already worn down from the longtime lack of sleep, my nagging sinus condition only made the trip even more miserable. I'd been on various medications by this time, and most recently, was treated for bronchitis.

I knew I'd receive the results from the CT scan that had been done before my birthday party, and I hoped they'd provide some answers. I

had previously sought the opinion of ER doctors, and Dr. Bowman had ordered a CT scan of my sinuses to better identify the problem. Keri and I felt hopeful that we'd finally get some answers so I could get better and get on with my life. More than anything, I just wanted to feel better, and to once again feel rested.

On the day of the scan, as I waited for the technician to complete the images, my mind had been on some issues at work and I was eager to get back to the office. Just taking time for the CT scan had aggravated me because it took me away from work. I knew though, that the scan would pinpoint the stubborn infection that had plagued me for months.

Back from my China trip, I was driving and preoccupied with thoughts of an upcoming meeting, when my cell phone rang. I tried to steady myself as I absorbed the results of my CT scan. It was like I'd been kicked in the stomach, and I tried to catch my breath.

"Yes, okay. Thank you, Doctor," I numbly replied as I hung-up.

It seemed so cruel – to both of us – that Keri was hundreds of miles away when I got the news on that day. I just had to talk to her as I tried to digest what I'd just heard.

As I shakily dialed my cell phone, it all seemed surreal, as if I were an observer looking at someone else's life that had just been dealt the blow of a lifetime. It couldn't possibly be *my* life or my *family's* life that had been affected by what I'd just heard. I was a husband, a father and a busy executive with responsibilities, deadlines and projects to complete. My life was going great and I simply had no time for such things as what the doctor had described!

We were all just happily celebrating my birthday and without a care in the world! Life had looked so perfect and promising that night! I thought. *How can all of it change in the blink of eye?*

"Hey!" Keri cheerfully answered, and I heard splashing and children's voices in the background that told me she was at swim practice with Max.

"It's a tumor! It's a tumor!" I screamed, as reality began to sink in for me.

I'm usually very excitable, so this reaction had seemed normal to Keri. She'd been expecting my call. The phone was silent, but I could feel Keri's shock on the other end as if she were right next to me in the room.

I learned later that as Keri sat poolside at Max's swim practice, next to a girlfriend, she'd tried to calmly absorb the news and keep it together as I screamed the word 'tumor' over and over. She told me later that it broke her heart that she couldn't hold me and hug me in that moment as she wrestled to find something reassuring to say as her own heart was breaking.

"But it's probably benign, right?" Keri eagerly asked as she tried to stay positive. "I'm sure it'll be benign, Rob."

"They'll know when they get in there and have a better look. They're scheduling me for a biopsy."

I focused on my work as I waited for the biopsy date to come. I wanted nothing more than to have the tumor removed, and then to hear that it was nothing to worry about. The doctor, however, explained that he'd intended to only biopsy a part of the tumor, as the first step.

Two weeks later, Keri's mom went to stay with the boys so that she could be with me in Rochester for the surgery. Keri kissed me one last time before the gowned nurses rolled me into the surgery unit where the biopsy would be performed.

"It'll be fine," she said with a smile, "I love you."

"Love you, too! See you soon."

The doctor went out to speak to Keri a little while later. She eagerly got up and walked to meet him, and my parents and my sister eagerly jumped up and followed her too.

As he removed his scrub cap from his head, the doctor said, "Well, I went ahead and removed it while I was in there. The tissue appears bloody and soft. Just looking at it, I don't think it'll be cancer, but we'll send it off just to be sure."

Keri drove me back to my parents' condo the day before Mother's Day; and she stayed by my side while I was on my back for the next 24 hours, per my doctor's orders. It felt odd to be together, in the master bedroom of the condo, because it had once been ours before we'd sold it to my parents. The surroundings were oddly familiar, and yet Keri and I had grown so much and gone through so many changes since when we'd first lived there.

We felt good two weeks later, and without a care in the world, as we arrived to get the official results of the biopsied tumor. Keri and I were laughing and joking when we walked into my doctor's office to get the results. The nurse showed us to an exam room, where I sat on the exam table and Keri took a seat in a chair across from me and against a wall.

The doctor walked in as we were laughing about something one of the boys had done. His face looked somber and serious as he held a clipboard in front of him. I studied his face, yet had no clue what he'd say to us, as he took a deep breath.

"The results are in," he said, "And it's not the diagnosis I expected — not at all. You have lymphoma."

It felt like I'd just been kicked in the stomach as the doctor's words plunged into me. Keri covered her mouth. Just the suffix 'oma' spelled *cancer*; and it was the one thing we hadn't expected to hear, not in a million years.

I took a deep breath and was ready to hear what we'd do about this obstacle that had been put in my path. As far as I was concerned, it was a hurdle, one I'd go over or even go through, but it wasn't going to block me forever.

"It'll be okay," the doctor told us, as he turned toward Keri, to outline what would happen next.

We walked out of the doctor's office and got in our car, completely changed from the happy, carefree couple we'd been just an hour earlier when we'd walked in. Keri drove us home while I called my parents. After I'd dialed the phone, she reached over and held my hand as we drove through traffic.

How can I tell them this? I thought while I waited for them to pickup. I was a parent, with sons of my own, and I could think of nothing worse that I might hear from my own children — no matter their age.

Dad didn't hear well over the phone, so I knew I'd have to speak loudly, which only made delivering the news more offensive and brutal. My heart raced and I took a deep breath as I waited.

"Dad?" I said loudly.

"Rob! Hi!"

"Dad, I have cancer."

"What?" Dad asked.

"Dad, I have *cancer!*" I said more loudly.

I felt the words hit my dad through the phone. It seemed so cruel to tell him my news. He'd always been the strong patriarch of our family, and

he and Mom had always had positive attitudes, no matter what. I knew he'd paused to digest what he'd just heard.

"It'll be fine, Rob," he said after a short silence. "Everything's going to be fine."

I needed that. I needed Dad's strength and his positivity in that moment, just as I'd needed my dad for other less significant problems over the years. He'd taken a little bit of the burden and put it on his own shoulders, just as he'd always done, and just like we'd all counted on him to do. Dad's shoulders were even bigger than I'd known.

Keri still held my hand, and she squeezed it as she drove us home. Sometimes words simply weren't needed, and this was one of those times. Our intertwined fingers said it all. I knew Keri would be with me for whatever lay ahead. For better or for worse, in sickness and in health, she'd be there.

5

Seasons

By Future Islands

My world had been forever altered and I knew I'd seen the last carefree time I would ever know. The calendar continued to change though, as did the seasons, while the world kept spinning. But with my cancer diagnosis, also came the reality that my fortieth birthday had been the last fun, carefree time I'd know for a long time – or maybe forever. It was as if there was 'the time before,' when everything seemed light, airy and positive, and 'the time after' when things were tenuous, scary and dark. My new world seemed uncertain and tentative, as I realized how life could change so drastically, and in less than a week. I wished we could go back to my happy, carefree birthday celebration, surrounded by those who meant so much to me. I'd have given anything to go back to that innocent time before I knew about the nasty disease that could steal my life away and take me from Keri and the boys.

How I wished we'd all been right when we at first had thought I simply had allergies or a persistent sinus infection. We'd never imagined the worst, never in a million years.

The new *c-word* seemed so daunting and uncertain. Like most things in life though, I decided to create an orderly plan, work that plan and get results. I drew strength from our family and friends who all came through for us, as I tackled cancer head-on.

When I began chemotherapy, Keri and the boys were still living in Grand Rapids, since the boys were still finishing school. Our house, that we were having built in Clarkston, was almost complete; and we were set to move in one month. I was with my parents at their condo. Keri's parents kept the boys for us so she could accompany me to the chemo treatments.

"You know you'd easily qualify to take leave from your job under the FMLA laws," a friend told me.

"I can work through the chemo," I said with optimism. "I'll make it work. I can do it!"

Keri was at my side as the chemo drugs dripped through an IV into my body. Dr. Howard had explained how chemo works and Keri and I read online about it too. Knowledge is power, and I wanted to know how this part of my plan would work. We knew the chemo drugs worked to stop or slow the growth of cancer cells, which grow and divide quickly. While attacking the cancerous cells though, the drugs can also harm the healthy cells that divide quickly, especially those that line the mouth and intestines and cause hair to grow. Damage to the healthy cells can cause multiple side effects, some of which are very uncomfortable. I wasn't sure exactly what to expect, but I'd heard and read stories of the various horrific side effects.

Thankfully, today's technology made it easier and more convenient to keep our family and friends updated on all that was going on in our world

during this time. People constantly called, sent emails and texts to find out how I was doing, and Keri did her best to reply to them as we moved through our new journey. Keri checked in with everyone via a text message in the earliest days of our unwanted adventure:

> *Hello everyone! Just had a chance to get back to all of you and let you know what's happening. Rob had a port put in and he received a dose of chemo. He took it like a champ, though he felt a little nauseated. Rob's spirits are good and his attitude is great, as usual. Thank you all for your thoughts and prayers!*

Keri and I tried to stay positive, talking and joking with the nurses and each other, as the invasive medicine dripped into my veins. While I waited for the session to end, my mind wandered to all the projects I'd been working on at the office. As vice president of New Business Development with Hydeswort, I'd worked to establish a New Business Team that included people in marketing, product management, social media, industrial design and product design. I implemented a New Product Process to be used companywide for future business ideas. I developed and implemented a new strategy for a first-to-market product in the outdoor products division that included legal, testing, sourcing, marketing, product development and branding.

My work life was busy and there was so much going on that I hated to even take time out for my chemo treatments. Keri and our family were all so great and I never went alone to chemo. One day, when Keri couldn't stay for the entire three-hour session, my sister Cindy came and sat with me.

If indeed there's 'strength in numbers,' they all did their best to lend me theirs as my own was challenged.

I quickly learned what to expect with the whole chemo process. We packed a cooler with Popsicles, cold drinks and fruits; and we passed time, as the chemo dripped into me, watching movies on my iPad. I knew it would be on day two following chemo when I'd feel feverish and nauseated, so when the chemo sessions finished, I tried to get as much done at work as possible before the debilitating side effects struck.

One day, while at chemo, I looked around at the other people in the room with me. Seeing all the other cancer patients lined up in their chairs, with IVs dripping into their arms, I realized how prevalent cancer really is today, and how it inflicts itself on unsuspecting people, interrupting lives, plans and families. We all had our own agendas, families, hopes and dreams; but we all shared one thing that united us, whether we'd wanted it to or not. We'd placed our faith in our doctors, said our respective prayers and desperately wanted to live for ourselves and for our families that needed us.

Cancer doesn't discriminate, as evidenced by people of all ages, from teenagers to the elderly, lined up around the chemo room that day. I wondered about all of them, their lives, their families and their individual worlds. There was a pretty teenaged girl who might have had cheerleading practice on any other day; an elderly gentleman whose white-haired wife sat beside him holding his hand, like she had probably done for half a century; a middle-aged Latina woman who talked on the phone about arrangements to pick up her kids from school; and all sorts of people of various ages and ethnicities. Each of them had lives, plans, dreams and responsibilities, just like I did. I only hoped each of them also had a strong, loving family and devoted friends, like I did, to support them and help them through the uncertain months that lay ahead.

The whole cancer thing had thrown a wrench into my orderly, responsible and predictable world. But I knew it was something I had to deal with so that I could again focus on my work. It would be an inconvenience, but I knew I'd get through it. I had to get through it. Keri and the boys were counting on me.

The first few chemo treatments went as well as could be expected. Our friends and family were our rocks during this time, pitching in and helping with the kids, accompanying me to chemo, coming to see me, and constantly keeping in touch.

I felt tired, of course, and as if I had hardly any energy. My world didn't stop though, and work called to me. In the mornings, I had my coffee, tried to muster the energy just to get in my car and dragged myself into my office. What I'd once done without thinking was by now, an exhaustive chore. Even the simplest of tasks zapped my energy and left me feeling withered and wasted. I hardly knew the guy whose tired eyes looked at me from my car's rearview mirror.

My boss, Walter, was unlike any I'd had before. He'd been employed in eight jobs, versus the three I'd had; and I wonder why. When he moved me to another area of the office building, I felt sure he was concerned about me and felt I threatened his position with the company. While I'd once worked on important projects with heavy responsibilities, my new role left me feeling unchallenged and as if I'd been given 'busy work' that would be best suited to less experienced new hires. Walter reported to Bruce, and I got along well with Bruce, but there was a chain of command to be respected, so I decided to just bide my time and go along with Walter's whims.

Since I'd always been very detail oriented, I documented all my appointments and logged my meetings. In an effort to dutifully keep my employer updated, I sent an email to Walter on July 11:

Walter –

Quick reminder… Next Monday, July 16th, I will be out of the office all day for Day One of the 2nd treatment of Chemo. On Day Two, Tuesday, July 17th, I'll need to leave by 2:30 for the second portion of the chemo. This treatment will be my 2nd out of 6 treatments, which will occur every three weeks. Approximately two weeks after the chemo is completed I will then begin 30 days of radiation. The plan is that cancer will be beaten, and all treatments will be complete by Halloween.

Thanks.

Rob Atteberry

6

Running Up that Hill

By Kate Bush

With all that had been going on lately, Keri and I were crazy busy. We had moved into our new home on July 2, less than a month after I'd started chemo. Instead of an exciting time, this particular summer seemed overwhelmingly busy, as our family tried to settle into our new home while I also battled cancer.

After a few weeks in our new home, we were still settling in. As if things couldn't get any more hectic, and just when I was sure there was no chance of any worse news than I'd already gotten, we received a phone call on July 30. My dad's brother, and my only blood-related uncle, Dale, had died of lung cancer.

"I've got to be in Missouri," I told Keri. "I've got to get to the funeral."

Keri had been getting the house organized, while tending to my needs and caring for the boys, since I wasn't of much help at this point. I don't know what I'd have done without her.

"I'll drive you," she said. "We'll go to Missouri, and the boys can stay here with my parents."

"I'll let them know at work," I said as Keri went to get our suitcases.

My stomach felt queasy and I was so exhausted as I dialed my boss to tell him I'd need to be gone for a couple days for our unexpected family emergency.

"Rob, do you really need to go?" my boss asked.

I hesitated as the crassness of his question sunk in, then I replied, "Ah, yeah. Yes, I really do. Our family is very close; he's my only blood-uncle and I need to be there."

As Keri drove us to Missouri, I fielded phone calls from my office and my employees, while she spent most of the time on her phone with my doctor as she tried to get a prescription sent to a St. Louis pharmacy near where we'd be staying. I was exhausted, but even worse were the painful mouth sores that were all over the inside of my mouth. I'd dealt with mouth sores throughout my treatment, but this time it was so much worse than ever before. It was incredibly painful to speak with thrush, or *Candidiasis*, the fungal infection that had spread throughout my mouth, another side effect of the chemo. I was so miserable as I took phone calls while Keri drove us to my Uncle Dale's funeral. Keri handed me Biotine gum to soothe and moisten my mouth, as I tried to talk to people from my office with a swollen, raw mouth full of canker sores.

"Rob, you can't keep this up," Keri urged. "Just let the calls go to voice mail."

But it would have bothered me not to respond and help people, since it was important for me to pull my weight, even with all I had going on.

As soon as we got to St. Louis, Keri drove us straight to the pharmacy to pick-up my prescription of liquid Nystatin, the generic for Bio-Statin,

which is an oral anti-fungal medication. We next went to the funeral home and then we went to dinner with my family, although I could barely keep my eyes open by this time. My mom hadn't seen me in six weeks because she and Dad had been at the lake. Mom was utterly shocked by how much weight I'd lost and how sickly I looked since she'd last seen me. I was too weak and tired to talk about much of anything, but the mouth sores prevented me from even trying. I just wanted nothing more than to get to the hotel and lie down.

When we got to the hotel later that night, I was completely exhausted and I'd begun to shake, possibly out of sheer exhaustion. The shaking that came with exhaustion was something that had been happening frequently in the last few weeks, so Keri and I had developed a routine to help me get through it. She'd climb into bed with me, spoon my body with hers and hold me tightly until her body heat finally stopped my uncontrolled shivering.

On this night, we resorted to the same routine. Finally, I fell asleep, as Keri held me and kept me warm. This scene had become a routine with us, because I was unable to control my own body temperature anymore.

Before dawn, I woke up and carefully got out of bed, so as not to wake Keri. I grabbed my laptop and went to the desk in our hotel room.

Hours later, when the alarm went off, Keri woke up and asked, "Rob? What are you doing?"

"I've got to get this stuff done before we leave for the funeral this morning," I said.

"What? How long have you been up?"

"I don't know — maybe three hours. I just want to get this work done before we leave for the funeral."

"Here you go," Keri said as she wrapped a blanket around my shoulders.

"I just need another hour or so, and then I'll be done here," I said.

We attended my uncle's funeral, and as I looked around at all the mourn-ers, I was even more convinced I'd dig in and fight my own cancer. It was too painful to even think of Keri and our boys without me. I was even more determined to fight the beast that threatened not only me, but also our whole family. The chemo was miserable and the side effects daunting. But just like a man would do anything for his wife and children, I vowed to do anything and everything to stay here with Keri and the kids. I popped another piece of Biotine gum into my mouth to sooth the festering mouth sores, and then I held Keri's hand again.

By this time, I'd had three rounds of chemo. The effects on my body were evident, and I hoped the chemo was working to annihilate the can-cer, which by now, I regarded as my opponent. I postured, both mentally and physically, to steel myself for the continuing battle that lay ahead. Since I'd been working, even through the chemo and its endless side effects, I felt comfortable about one thing: *my job*. Not only did I need my job, but I also needed my health insurance if I was to continue my fight against the cancer that threatened to take me from my family. For this reason, I continued to do my job, no matter how sick I felt or how weak I became.

"What can I get you?" Keri asked one morning as I sat at the bar in the kitchen, dressed for work, but so exhausted.

"Nothing. I'm just trying to get the energy to get in the car."

I'd gotten to the point where I knew what to expect and how to pace myself to find every ounce of energy throughout my day. If I got dressed, then made it to the kitchen, I knew I could sit down and regroup for ten minutes, so I could then go outside and get into my car. Even the simplest, most mundane tasks became exhaustive and draining.

"Go! Go! Go!" I mentally willed myself again and again, when I didn't think I could take another step.

As I trudged into work, the words filled my head, even as I counted down the remaining steps into office. I half-smiled at people on the way in, careful not to waste energy with conversation or break my stride.

"Go! Go! Go!" I silently repeated until I finally got to my desk and sat down to catch my breath as I read the morning's emails and messages.

I hated the fact that I felt so weak. I resented that my body had betrayed me.

Where was the old Rob? I often wondered. *Where was the guy who could run for miles? Where was the guy who competed in triathlons and who always felt great? Would I ever see him again or was he gone for good?*

The guy who I met at the mirror each morning looked gaunt, with hollow eyes and dull, pale skin. He'd lost all his hair, even his eyebrows and eyelashes. He looked skinny and sick, more like a shell of a man, than the guy who I'd known my whole life.

"You're always handsome to me," Keri reminded me, as she circled her arms around me from the back, as I looked in the mirror. "And I love you."

Her positive attitude and constant affirmations got me through some of my toughest days. She was always there for me, beside me every step of the way. I'd always loved her, but when we faced down cancer together, we

became even closer. On those days when I couldn't find the strength, she gave me hers, until I could gather my own again. I think we both began to understand the true meaning of marriage and all it meant. My 'cute Keri' was even stronger than I'd ever known.

Chemo Number Four was on August 6. By this time, I knew what to expect and how to pace myself for what would happen. Keri was with me, as always, when the poison dripped into my veins, ready to do battle with the cancer and to stand with me as we defeat our enemy. She and I talked and joked, and as always, I was constantly amazed by the strength of my wife.

Keri's positive attitude became my rock and helped me to stay strong, even in the face of uncertainty. We both knew of all the possible sides effects and that many cancer patients experienced anxiety and depression during and after chemo treatments. With Keri by my side, it was easier to ward off at least *this* side effect.

After Chemo Four, I paced myself and waited a couple days for the exhaustion, mouth sores, lack of appetite and nausea to hit. It had become a predictable cycle by this time and I knew what to expect, just as sure as I knew the sun would rise each morning.

When it became apparent that I simply couldn't eat though, Keri insisted we get to the hospital.

"It'll pass. It always does. I can get through it," I told her.

Keri kept in constant touch with the chemo nurse. She dealt with each side effect as it came, one at a time, or several at a time.

I went to the office during this bout of side effects. As I talked with vendors and employees on the phone, I swallowed down the rising nausea, as I fought to focus on our conversations. I felt constantly cold and

I couldn't stop my body from shivering. In between calls, reports and emails, I went into the bathroom to put cold water on my face, though it never helped.

It got to the point that I could only eat soft, breakfast foods. Keri made me lots of pancakes and eggs, and I ate plenty of Gummy Bears.

By August 15, both Keri and I were surprised that the side effects hadn't relented at all. I grew weaker by the hour, as I tried to continue to plow through my work, but I was determined not to miss a beat at work and to keep up with my responsibilities. I was also running a low grade fever. My doctor advised me not to worry about and to alert him if it spiked.

It was now, when I began to really feel the effects of what was happening inside my body, thanks to the chemo treatments. Since I was so weak, Keri let our friends and family know what was going on:

Although Rob's been handling this like a champ, he's dealing with some side effects from the chemo, namely fatigue, mouth-sores and thrush. He has no appetite and finds it difficult to eat or talk because of the painful mouth sores. He says he feels 'funky' – his words, not mine. He's spending time on his computer and trying to keep up with his work and I wish he'd rest more, but then we all know how he can be!

Not only did I feel sick, but I also knew Walter wanted me at work, even though I could barely even hold my head up. Since I've always been a dependable person with a good work ethic, it really bothered me that I was too sick to go into work. As a result, it was impossible to rest as my mind whirled and buzzed with all the responsibilities that called to me from the office.

In hindsight, I'd realize it would have been best for me to take a leave of absence from work, since I'd definitely have qualified for it based on my

circumstances. But I really thought I could work through the chemo, and just keep going as usual.

I really thought that if I could just rest and regain my strength, that I'd get through it. Our yearly vacation to Lake of the Ozarks was quickly approaching and I wasn't sure how I'd find the energy to make the eleven hour drive.

"Listen, Keri, you and the boys just go on to the lake as planned," I said. "I'll be fine here."

"I'm not leaving you like this!" she insisted as she looked at me like I was crazy.

"No, the boys have been looking forward to going to the lake. You all go ahead. Seriously, I'll be fine. You can't do anything for me here anyway. I'm just going to lie down and rest, so the peace and quiet here will be perfect for me."

Although it took some convincing, Keri finally relented and she took the boys to meet my parents at Lake of the Ozarks, for the regularly scheduled family trip. Since I had so little energy and I felt totally drained, I went to bed and hoped I'd feel rested later. I slept fitfully, but I got up and went to work in the morning and then to a scheduled check-up with my doctor. My white blood cell count was drastically low.

"You need to remain isolated for rest of the week, Rob," the doctor advised. "I mean totally isolated – no work, no public places, not even tap water for you. You can only drink bottled water."

At the end of the doctor visit, I felt even more exhausted. I went home and went straight to bed. When I woke up hours later, I felt even sicker still, if that was even possible.

By the next day, I felt worse and worse. The thermometer confirmed my suspicions: *101.1.* When I took my temperature again later, it was by then over *102.*

Keri sent me a text: *How are you feeling?*

I sent her a photo of the thermometer beside me.

That doesn't look good, Keri texted back.

I'll be ok. I love you, I replied.

I'd learn later that Keri had phoned her friend, Dana, and asked her to bring over cases of bottled water and some Gummy Bears, because that was the only thing for which I had an appetite.

I went back to bed, pulled the covers up around my neck and instantly fell asleep again. A little while later, I heard the doorbell ring at our house's side entrance. I was white as a ghost and my breathing was shallow and labored as I opened the door.

"Wow! You look awful, Rob!" Dana said when she saw me. "Ker's worried about you, so I wanted to come by and check on you. I think we should go to the hospital."

Hours later, I was still in the hospital's waiting room when Dana talked on the phone with Keri.

"Keri, Rob looks really bad." Dana said. "He's pale and his breathing is shallow. It's scary. I'll stay with him until he's admitted. You should take the next flight home. I'll call you again in a few hours."

After several tests, the doctor came in to talk to me.

"You have neutropenia due to the chemo," the doctor confirmed. "When you become neutropenic, your white blood count is abnormally low; and you're more susceptible to bacterial infections as a result. It's hard for the body to fight off infection. It can become life threatening, depending upon the duration. You've also got pneumonia and that's why you're having difficulty breathing. It's a good thing you got to the hospital.

We'll need to keep you isolated for a few days, get some IV antibiotics going; and we'll try to figure out what's causing the infection."

Keri took the next flight home and her friends, Dana and Jill, picked her up at the airport at 1:00am and brought her to the hospital. My parents stayed at the lake with the boys so Keri could be with me.

"I need to use your laptop," I told her, minutes after she'd arrived.

"For what? You're supposed to be resting."

"I've got to let them know at work what's going on."

Keri brought me my laptop and as I read my emails, I opened one from my boss.

"I've got a meeting in a couple days," I told Keri as she sat beside my hospital bed.

"You can hardly stand up!"

"Maybe I'll be better by tomorrow."

When my boss read the email I'd sent him, he replied to me with 'I'm here for you, Rob! Let me know if there's anything you need."

The doctors kept me in the hospital for three days, and then sent me home.

"Bed rest, Rob. That's what you need," the doctor reminded me as he signed the release form. "We're not going to do the fifth or sixth chemo. Our goal is not to kill you! Go home and rest."

Keri shot me a knowing glance and shook her head.

After my three days in the hospital, I thought I felt good enough to go home; and after a couple more days, I even had a little bit of strength back.

Keri wanted me to take more time though, to rest and to get stronger; but I felt like I needed to get back to work. We later learned that an abscessed tooth had caused the elusive infection that had sent me to the hospital.

"How can you go into work, Rob?" she asked one morning. "You're exhausted after just getting dressed. You can barely even stand up."

"I'll be okay. Really."

A few hours later, Keri called me at work to see how I was doing.

"Fine," I said, "But I'm freezing. I just can't get warm, no matter what I do."

An hour later, Keri showed up at my office with a sweater for me.

"You need to be at home and in bed," she said, as she kissed me good-bye, and I put on the sweater.

"I'll see you tonight. Kiss the boys for me," I told her.

Although I felt worse than I'd ever felt in my life, I knew I needed to pull my weight at work. Since I had cancer, I was certain that I could not lose my job. My family was counting on me; and I knew I had to keep my health insurance, if I planned to continue treatment.

The next morning, I woke up and paced myself as I dressed, rested at the bar in our kitchen and got in my car. Keri walked me outside and kissed me goodbye, but the look on her face told me she didn't approve of me going to work so soon.

I made it through the day, and then the next one too, but on August 27, I called my boss to tell him I'd be working from home on that day, because I was still sick. The next day, I did the same thing. Although I'd worked from home before, when I was sick from the chemo, by this time, I'd missed being physically in the office a total of 23 days between May and August.

The next morning, after I talked to HR, I sent an email to document our conversation for Hydeswort and I copied my boss, as always:

Rick –

Attached is the link to the Cancer calendar, along with the detail below. Access is available for this calendar to you, Walter and Scott. Anne also had access while she was still here. The calendar is kept up to date with all appointments, days off and information.

In addition, I attached the "days off" spreadsheet that we reviewed today.

Thanks for your time, and as always I will keep you up to speed on any changes.

Rob Atteberry

7

The Way We Get By

By Spoon

In addition to the long list of unpleasant side effects from the chemo, I also had some additional teeth issues too, another result of the chemo's assault on my body. I'd always dealt with teeth problems; but the chemo had further weakened my teeth and gums, which eventually led to a root canal and another new crown, as if I needed even one more thing to deal with at the time. I took it in stride though and went through each day one at a time.

The month of September went by and my body slowly began to heal from the chemo that had invaded it in an effort to kill off the bad cancer cells. I *thought* things were progressing just as they should and I'd worked my way through the exhaustion, the hair loss and the fact that no foods tasted good anymore. I tried to take it all in stride.

On October 1, I kissed Keri goodbye and headed off to the office, like I'd done countless times before. My mind was on all the items on that day's calendar, and I made mental notes of people I needed to call and things I needed to do, while I headed to my new office, where Walter had recently relocated me.

Minutes later, seated at my desk, and as I looked at a report on my computer screen, my intercom buzzed.

"Rob, I need to talk to you," Walter said.

"Sure. Be right there."

Thirty minutes later, I was in my car again and driving home in the early morning sun. I felt like I'd been hit head-on by a train that I hadn't seen coming.

"Hey!" Keri said cheerfully as she answered my phone call.

"I'm on my way home," I said, feeling bruised and shell-shocked.

"Now? Why? Do you feel okay, Rob?" she panicked.

"They let me go, Keri. Walter just fired me. I'll see you in a few minutes and tell you about it."

As I pulled into our neat, manicured neighborhood, the grass was still wet with the morning dew. A woman walked behind a baby stroller and another woman jogged along the street with earphones in her ears. It dawned on me that their worlds were calm, predictable and peaceful, while my own had just completely imploded with no warning.

I parked in our driveway and stoically went inside.

"What....?" Keri asked as she dried her hands with a dishtowel and came over to me. "Why? I don't under....."

I walked into my home office and Keri followed me.

"Walter and Rick said my area is being reorganized and so they had to let two people go. Jim and I were it. Some other employees are being merged with another department," I explained, still trying to digest it all myself.

"I can't believe it! You've been killing yourself for that company, even since you got sick!" Keri said as she hugged me where I numbly sat at my desk surrounded by shelves of thousands of neatly organized CDs.

"I don't get it either."

"Wait a minute, Rob. This is crazy.... How can they let you go? I mean right *now*, just as you're going through cancer treatment?"

"I know. I'll have to cancel the radiation treatments that are scheduled to start October 20."

"You can't do that!"

"I won't have insurance though, Keri."

"We'll find a way," she said.

"I just need to work it all out. I know we'll get by," I assured her. "I just don't want to tap into our savings, especially if I don't have a job."

"What did you say to them when they told you, Rob?"

"I said 'I'll be talking to you,' and then I got up and left. My legs felt like lead weights as I walked out of there."

The rest of that first day of October was a blur, as I played the bizarre scene over and over in my mind, and tried to make sense of what had happened to abruptly upend my world. Cancer had come into my life abruptly and with no warning, and so had being let go from my job with no notice and at the worst possible time.

My stomach was twisted with anger, resentment and absolute shock that Bruce, my onetime friend, could have possibly sanctioned my firing at any time — much less a time when I was fighting for my life and battling cancer. Bruce had brought me up in the ranks with Gechsmin; and then he'd asked me to come to Hydeswort and to work under Walter.

The whole thing continued to make no sense to me and I felt like I'd been kicked in the stomach.

We had hit rock bottom, and as the husband and father in our family, it was up to me to take control and fix things for us. I'd have given anything to have the energy to work on my newest problem, but I was having difficulty just wrapping my head around what had happened to me. I hadn't seen it coming and I felt like I'd been sucker-punched and I still couldn't fully catch my breath.

My emotions ran the gamut. One minute I was fuming and furious, and the next I felt worried and anxious. I'd done what was expected of me. I'd been a reliable, productive employee for Hydeswort, just like I'd been in any other position I'd ever held. It was just in my makeup to be dependable and responsible, and I really presumed that if I'd held up my end of the employment deal, that my employer would naturally do the same.

Wasn't that how it was supposed to be?

We had money in the bank, but I knew radiation would be expensive. In addition to all the financial considerations, I was left with so many questions about why my job had been summarily stripped away from me, like a defender might strip a football from the ball carrier. But I wasn't in a football game, and I certainly didn't have the bank account of a professional athlete. I was but a typical, run-of-the-mill, middle-class guy who presumed his employer would return his loyalty and humanity, especially at the worst time of his life.

The non-stop questions plagued me, although most of them were rhetorical and so they'd never be answered:

Did Walter see me as a potential threat, especially since he'd already had so many jobs over the span of his own career?

Was he already trying to find a way to get rid of me when he'd moved me into a smaller, unimportant office across the hall?

Why had I been given the boring, innocuous project of working on fabric planters, when I'd successfully handled much more high-profile projects?

Was I already sick with cancer when I went to Hydeswort?

Did I have cancer when I was with Tendlart?

Would I ever get any answers?

I'd be lying if I said I wasn't concerned, even somewhat frightened, about how to proceed at this point in our lives. I had worked so hard, and for so many years, to get our family to a certain standard of living. Keri and I were proud of the spacious home we'd built for our boys, and the fact that we could give them the lives they deserved. My cancer had been just a stumbling block that I was sure I'd overcome. But being unemployed had never been something I'd expected, since I thought I'd done everything right. I'd come to work, even when I was so sick; I'd worked from home to pull my weight for the company; I'd made myself available, day and night, no matter what, and I'd been a team player from Day One.

"Mom and Dad think I should go on long-term disability," I told Keri.

"Well, I'm also getting a job," Keri proclaimed one day. "I'm going back to teaching."

"No, not yet. I'll figure it out."

"I was going to go back to teaching anyway," she insisted, "And the twins are older, so it's time."

"Okay, I'll look into long-term disability while you see about a teaching job."

We'd always been a team, Keri and I, but this time it felt different. I wasn't leading the team like I'd always done, and she was shouldering more of the burden than made me comfortable. To make matters worse, we had no play book either.

"We'll get through this," Keri said as she hugged me. "You'll see."

While I contemplated things, Keri sent an email to her best girlfriends:

Hi Girls,

Sorry I've been hard to reach for a couple days. Things are insane right now. Rob and I are still trying to digest what's happened. I really just don't get it. He gave his all to his job – even when he was so sick that he could barely even stand. On the days when I begged him not to go in to the office, he said he 'had a responsibility to the company' and that he'd be fine.' What kind of people would fire a guy who's dealing with cancer? It seems heartless, at the very least. Rob seems lost right now. He's always worked so hard and he was proud of how far he's come and at such a young age. It's like they pulled the rug out from under him at the very worst time of him life, and with no warning at all. I just can't believe this happened. I'm sure we'll be okay, we just need to take some time and figure out what to do. Anyway, thanks for letting me vent. Gotta run...

-Keri

I delayed my upcoming radiation appointments and decided to consult an attorney. He told me that nine out of ten times, a sick employee's employer puts him on long-term disability in similar situations. When I talked to Hydeswort though, I was told disability wasn't a possibility for

me, since I'd already been removed from the company and severed as an employee on any level.

So, I was fired, less than 24-hours ago; and they've got no record that I even worked there? I furiously thought.

I felt overwhelmed and abandoned, like a fish floundering on a dock and gasping for breath. So much of my identity and how I viewed myself in the world was tied up in my corporate identity. My new world seemed dark, uncertain and foreboding as I planned my next steps. Keri, who is usually so calm and even tempered, was angry with the company and continued to worry about my health.

"What they did to you is wrong – it's just plain *morally wrong*. But the most important priority right now is for you to start radiation. We need to get you well."

While I dealt with my health and the impending disaster brought on my employer, Keri maintained our family and our home life. Meanwhile, my attorney contacted Hydeswort about our intent to sue for my wrongful termination. I found it odd that Bruce and Walter denied even having known that I had cancer.

"Not only did they know," I told my attorney, "But Walter and I even exchanged emails on it. I'll give you copies of the correspondence."

Because I was so grateful to be done with chemo and I just wanted to get on with my life, I moved on to the next stage of my battle and began radiation treatments. At least I had the insurance concerns handled.

Radiation treatments turned out to be an intense experience. On the first day, I lay still on a table while several technicians fitted a soft piece of plastic around my head and molded an exact replica of my head and face.

This whole process is so bizarre, I thought. *How did I get to this point?*

I'd wondered, at least a thousand times in the many months prior, how I could possibly be dealing with cancer and all it entails. It just didn't seem possible that I'd gone through all I had; and that I was still ensnared in cancer's grasp. But I was determined to fight each battle — and to *win* the war.

The radiation treatments required that I go to my doctor's office at the same time each day for 21 straight days. The entire process, from the minute I arrived, only took 20 minutes, with the actual radiation lasting less than five minutes in total. The radiologist decided to administer the lowest possible dosage, since the targeted area was so close to my brain.

Each day, I lay still, on a cold, hard table in a still, sterile room, with the specially made plastic mask fitted over my head. Without moving, my eyes watched as the gigantic machine navigated slowly around my head.

Stay positive! I silently reminded myself, as I thought of Keri and the boys. *You've got this! You'll beat it! Go! Go! Go!*

I willed myself to stay positive and hopeful, although deep inside, I felt entirely overwhelmed. Still though, it gave me such comfort to know Keri waited faithfully in the other room for my treatment to finish; and that I'd again see her reassuring smile in just a couple minutes. 'Cute Keri' had a strength within her that was both a blessing and powerful source of strength to me.

I thought often of the wedding vow that reminds us we promise to be there for our partner 'in both sickness and in health.' When I'd married Keri, I could've never imagined there would come a time when *I* would need to lean on *her*; but she was there for me, steadfast and strong, when I needed her most.

On the days when Keri was busy with the kids, my dad took me to my radiation treatments. With Dad there, I felt a different kind of strength, a different sort of empowerment and encouragement that was almost

tangible. It was as if Dad had willed his strength and positivity to me when I needed it most; and yet, no words were needed between father and son.

Boys always look up to their fathers as their first heroes, often trying to emulate and imitate the strength and character of their dads. While I may have been a grown man, and even a father, myself, Dad would never know how much it meant to have him there with me.

Since we'd never before been through radiation, none of us had any idea what a big event it is when a patient completes his final radiation treatment. We later learned, however, about the traditional 'bell ringing ceremony' that signifies a patient's last treatment. For my last treatment though, I ended up driving myself to the appointment, unaware of how this milestone is celebrated.

Immediately after my last radiation, the kind nurses walked me back to the waiting room and then cheered and clapped as I rang the bell that marked my final treatment. I felt hopeful as I drove away from that last appointment.

When I got home later that day, Keri had a big bunch of balloons and a candy bar bouquet waiting for me, in celebration of the end of my treatments. I was amazed that she'd been so thoughtful in the wake of all she'd been going through, but then again, that's Keri, "the nicest person I've ever met!"

When my radiation ended, I then had scans done to see if the chemo and radiation had worked. The word "remission" had never had more meaning, nor sounded so good when we heard it.

8

A Pain That I'm Used To

By Depeche Mode

New Year's 2013 had brought with it the hope and promise of a brighter future like no year before it. Keri and I felt like we'd battled the cancer beast and had won. Unbeknownst to me at the time though, Keri was still worried.

I can't put my finger on it, but Rob seems a little out of it sometimes. Maybe it's a bit of depression, which I know affects some people when they fight cancer. I just miss his smile and his sense of humor around the house, Keri texted to a friend.

Even though I'd been officially declared in remission by February, Keri still bore the brunt of caring for our four boys. She and I presumed I was still fatigued from all I'd been through in the last few months.

We wanted to bring some fun and laughter back into the house, so we got a puppy for the boys in February. Like all puppies do, ours had the occasional accident while being housebroken. What was out of the ordinary though, was my strange lackluster response to the puppy's accident one day, though Keri would tell me about it later.

"Rob, what's wrong with you?" Keri asked one afternoon when she came into the family room.

"What do you mean?" I asked in an unaffected monotone voice.

"The puppy, Rob! The puppy threw up on the floor and the boys are running all around, and you're not even paying attention to any of it!" she said. "What's going on?"

I heard her voice, but her words, nor her exasperation, registered with me. The house could have been on fire, for all I knew, but I had literally *no reaction* – to anything or anyone – by this time. I was physically there, but mentally and cognitively, I felt trapped inside my physical form, and unable to participate in life. The 'Old Rob' would have instantly sprung into action, cleaned-up the puppy's mess, reprimanded him and taken control of the boys as they ran around the house. 'The New Rob' couldn't seem to connect the dots to respond to anything as he merely observed life as a silent spectator.

It's like he has no reaction – to anything! He sits and stares at the TV, but he's not really watching it. It's as if he's here, but he's NOT here. He sleeps constantly! He doesn't even smile anymore! It's like he's tuned out and shut off from everything! Something's very wrong! I'm really worried, Keri texted to Cindy.

As I slept away my days or sat stoically and unaffected day after day, Keri cared for the boys and handled our family's needs. In addition to all that, she gave me my medications, prepared food for me when I felt like eating and helped me to do everything – and I mean *everything*. Keri bathed the boys and tucked them into their beds each night; and then she helped me

to walk upstairs, helped me take a shower and then tucked me into bed too. Basically, Keri had five Atteberry boys that she cared for, but one of us was old enough to vote.

She soon insisted that I see a doctor to find out what was wrong with me. I'm sure her heart was broken, since she'd basically lost her husband, but Keri tried to stay focused, even with all the stress and responsibilities she carried at the time.

"It's PTSD," the doctor diagnosed. "It happens sometimes after people go through cancer treatment. Plus, he lost his job, and that was a big part of his identity and how Rob related to the world and his place in it. We can prescribe some antidepressants. I'd also like to send him for a sleep study to see if he's getting adequate oxygen while sleeping. If he's not, that explains why he's so tired. We'll take care of him. He'll be fine."

The doctor also suggested I see a therapist to talk about how I'd been feeling. Keri had a friend from high school who was a therapist specializing in treating cancer patients, so she made me an appointment.

I've started keeping notes about what Rob is doing, Keri texted to my sister. *It's weird, almost like he's looking thru me, not AT me. It's like he's physically here, but not really HERE. He'll be with your parents at the lake soon. Let's see what they think.*

Keri continued to try and engage me in conversation and to get some sort of response from me, other than a bland one-word reply. I was no longer able to drive by this point, so Keri did all the driving. This decision had come about one day when I'd been driving and had pulled into our subdivision, then just 'stopped' in the middle of the entrance, for no obvious reason.

"Rob, are you going to keep driving?" Keri asked from the passenger seat.

"Uh, oh, yeah," I replied.

That episode, coupled with other things she'd noticed, had Keri concerned. She handled all the boys' needs and helped me too, as she continued to worry that something just wasn't quite right with the husband she'd known.

Even I realized I'd ceased communicating with people, although I couldn't articulate my concerns. When I did speak, it was such an effort; and even then, Keri could only hear me if she leaned in and put her ear next to my mouth.

"I'm sorry I'm not talking much," I said, a few times. "I don't know why."

The sleep study revealed nothing. My oxygen levels were adequate when I slept, according to the findings of the study, so that wasn't the source of any problem.

"Oh, he'll snap out of it," the doctor told her when she talked to him. "Give the medication time to work. It has to build up in Rob's system and it's got a residual effect that multiplies over time. I'm sure he'll be just fine. You've both been through a lot in the last year. Give it some time."

Keri grew more and more concerned with each passing day. She talked with her friends and our family and emailed with everyone about what had been happening:

Hi All-

Sorry for the blanket mass email. It's been another long day and I just got the kids to bed, so it's late. Things aren't getting any better; in fact, Rob seems worse. It's definitely more than depression. We were outside today in the yard, and he lost his balance and fell over again for the third time. He was just standing there and he toppled over. That's not

depression. It seems like the doctors are completely missing it and I'm getting more worried. Thanks for checking in on him. I'll let you know if we learn anything new.

-Keri

When I went to the lake to stay with my parents in May, it gave Keri a welcome break. I didn't know it, but she had talked with my parents and she'd asked them to observe me and make notes, just as she'd done.

"I see what you mean. He's not talking as much, he's walking funny and one of his shoulders is drooped. I wonder if maybe he's had a stroke," my mom said to Keri after she'd spent some time with me. "I've looked up the symptoms on the Internet, and it really seems like it might be a stroke."

"Possibly," Keri replied. "I just don't know, Diane; but he's not himself – not at all. I really miss the old Rob. I'll go with him to his next appointment with the therapist, and I'll tell her what we've talked about."

Keri knew my mom must have been concerned, because Mom had researched my symptoms online. Our family jokingly refers to my mom as 'Dr. Atteberry,' because she constantly researches symptoms and tries to diagnose family members with her 'Web MD' findings. It's one of the things we love about Mom; she would go to the ends of the earth for her kids. Her research was Mom's way of doing all she could to help Keri and me at the time.

When it was time for my next appointment with the therapist, Keri accompanied me. I sat quietly and emotionless as the two of them discussed my behavior. I watched their mouths move and I heard their voices, but what they said didn't really register with me at all. I was merely a mute, contented onlooker while the two women talked about me. Still undiagnosed, I was basically trapped inside a failing, diminishing shell of a body, and time wasn't on my side.

"Look, Keri," the therapist said, "I've been reading about PSTD, and Rob *doesn't* have the symptoms of PTSD. I think it's something physical that's going on with him."

"We're supposed to go on a family trip next week," Keri told her. "It's a Disney cruise with the whole family. Should we still go?"

"I think you can take him. They'll have a doctor on board the ship; but keep an eye on him and don't leave him alone until we can figure this thing out."

Our family of six, my parents and my sister, her husband and their kids all went to Florida to set sail on the Disney cruise. I was very quiet and entirely exhausted, even from the moment we set foot on the cruise ship. The boys danced and excitedly enjoyed the bon voyage party on deck as the ship pulled out of port. Just watching them made me tired, but I presumed my body hadn't yet bounced back from the chemo and all I'd be through in the last months. I was quiet, and I didn't have the energy to make conversation, nor the desire to engage with people.

After breakfast the next day, I sat at the pool with my family, but was too exhausted to do anything else. I went back to our cabin for a nap and I was asleep in no time.

"Hey," Keri said as she rubbed my back, "Wake up, Rob. It's time for dinner."

"Dinner?" I asked. "How long was I sleeping?"

"Since 1:00. It's after 6:00 now. Are you hungry?" she asked.

"A little."

"Well, we're going to meet everyone in the dining room in thirty minutes."

Even a shower didn't help to energize me, and I was more fatigued than ever after I had dressed for dinner. Just getting ready for dinner had worn me out. Keri took my hand and led me from our cabin and into the hall and then guided me toward the elevators. I quietly walked beside her, and was glad she was leading the way. I'd learn later that it broke her heart to take my hand, as if I were one of our boys, but in front of me she was nothing but loving and strong.

The boys happily entertained each other during dinner, but the adults around our table seemed more quiet than usual, as they looked at me and then glanced toward one another. I was too exhausted to ask what was going on, nor did I really care at the time. Dinner seemed to take so long, and I was relieved when the waiter came to remove all the dessert and coffee dishes. I could barely hold my eyes open, and I told Keri I needed to go to bed.

"I'll walk back to the room with you," Keri said as she took my hand, "And then I'll come back and join the others on the deck."

"We'll take the boys with over to the Kids' Club," Diane offered. "You two go ahead."

When I was back in bed again, Keri tucked me in and then she went and found our family on the upper deck. They were all seated around a table and having drinks under the stars.

"The boys are at the Kids' Club," my mom told Keri. "We'll go back for them in a little while."

"Okay, thanks."

Keri sipped the drink they'd ordered for her and then she sadly said, "He's getting worse."

"We can tell," my sister, Cindy, agreed. "We've all been talking about it."

"I'm so worried," Keri said. "Something's just not right. This isn't depression. It's not PTSD. *What's* going on with him? Rob just keeps saying he's tired, but that's not it either. He's got an appointment with his oncologist on the day after we get back. Hopefully, we can get some answers."

The next morning, we all got off the ship and went ashore for an excursion. I followed our group, uncertain of where we were going, and not sure I really cared. It was as if I were on autopilot as my legs moved in sync with theirs — left, right, left, right. I stopped when my family did, and then I silently resumed my robotic pace alongside them.

Back on the ship, I took a nap again and awoke to find Keri curled up in a chair and writing in her journal.

"Hey. Whatcha doing?" I asked.

"Just writing about our day so I don't forget anything."

"Okay, I'm going to sleep a little longer."

Keri went back to her writing as the sun set outside:

What is going on with Rob? I handed our passports to him,
so he could hand them to the guy as we got back on the

ship, but he's so robotic, like he's not really here and engag-
ing with people. His dad had to help him and guide him all
day, saying 'Walk here, Rob; turn here; sit here' all day.
I'm terrified that the old Rob is gone, but I'm even more
scared that something awful is happening and the doctors
haven't identified it. This was not the vacation I'd imag-
ined — not at all.

While I slept, Keri went to my parents' cabin and found Cindy and her husband there. Everyone looked concerned and it was clear they'd all been talking about me.

"It's like his sense of humor is completely gone," Keri agreed. "He doesn't engage with anyone like he used to, not even the boys."

My mom and my sister fought back tears.

"It's like.... Like he's a zombie," Keri added. "I even miss arguing with him. I miss his Type-A personality and how he'd freak out over the smallest things."

My dad went to hug her and said, "Well, let's make the best of it and then we'll talk to the doctors when we get home again."

Everyone continued to accommodate me during our family trip. Because I was always so tired, they had to leave activities early to get me back to my cabin so I could take naps and we'd even eat dinner earlier than usual, so I could get to bed. Thankfully, we had family with us, because I was unable to interact with our boys myself.

After a couple more days at sea, our family was back in Florida and at Universal Studios in Orlando. Keri videotaped our family as we walked

around and went on the various rides throughout the day. My legs felt like lead and I stumbled at times, as I tried to keep pace with everyone and also keep my balance. The boys had a good time though, as our family enjoyed the Florida sunshine.

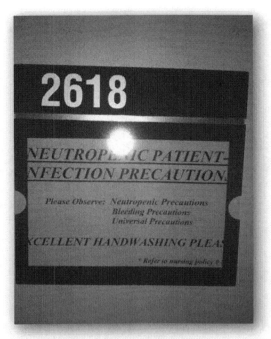

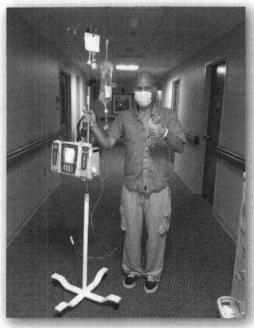

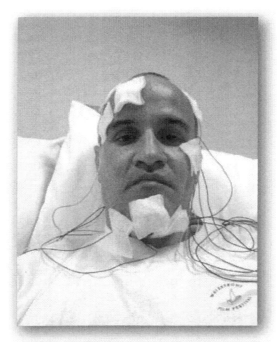

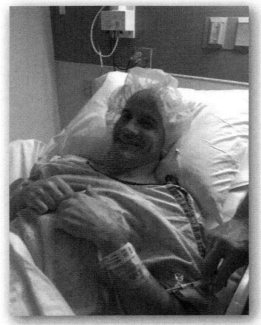

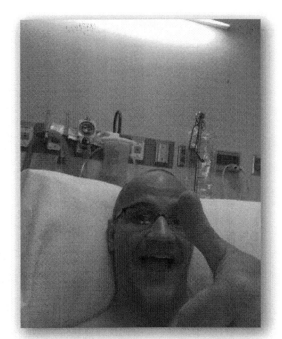

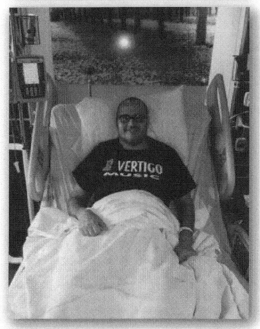

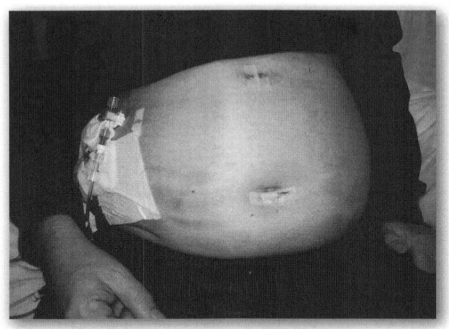

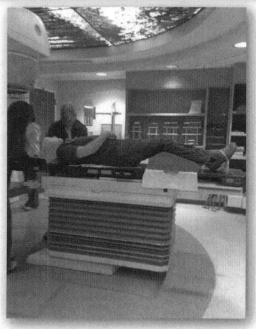

9

Everything Is Wrong

By Interpol

Back at home again, several days later, Keri told my mom she had been taking the video of our trip to show to my oncologist.

"Here," my mom said, "Take this letter too. I'm Rob's mother and I've known him all his life. A mother always knows when something's not right with her children. The doctor may have his M.D., but I've got my M.O.M. and many more years of experience in knowing my son. I want that doctor to hear from me while he views Rob on the videotape you're taking to him!"

Keri and I visited my oncologist and Keri immediately insisted he view the videotape and read my mom's detailed letter of the changes she saw in me. I'd never seen Keri be so forceful, pushy and insistent. She'd always been the polite, nice, mannerly one, so her demeanor was entirely out of character as I watched quietly.

The doctor viewed the video that showed me trying to keep my balance as my shoulder drooped and I stumbled a few times while I shuffled along. "I see what you mean," the doctor said.

"Our therapist said she doesn't believe he has PTSD," Keri explained to the doctor as she pushed the therapist's report closer to him.

"Has he had an MRI done of his brain?"

"No," Keri replied, "Just a PET Scan."

"Well, that wouldn't show his brain," the doctor confirmed.

"What?! I thought PET scans also show what's happening in the brain! Why have we not checked his brain?" Keri questioned.

"We will now. I will schedule an appointment immediately," the doctor said.

I observed their exchange, as if silently watching a tennis match from the sideline. I heard their voices volley back and forth, and yet their comments weren't entirely registering with me. But I trusted that Keri would handle things, and in a few minutes I followed her out of the office and back to our car.

"We're going to have an MRI done, Rob," Keri explained. "Maybe we'll get some answers."

Two days later, the MRI was done in the morning. Hours later, Keri and I were in the car and she was driving our boys home from a trampoline center in town. With the boys buckled in back, Keri drove along as her cell phone rang.

"Are you driving?" the doctor asked her.

"Yes," I heard her answer into the phone.

"Well, pull over if you can, Keri."

I watched as Keri pulled our Suburban off the road, put the gearshift in park, found a pad and pen in the console under her right elbow, and then got out. She was in front of the car with the phone to her ear as she wrote on the pad and leaned on the car's hood as cars whizzed by. I couldn't hear what she said, but her expression looked concerned and her eyes looked sad.

A couple minutes later, Keri opened the driver's door and got behind the wheel again. The pad was in a cup holder between the front seats. I watched her and I knew she seemed anxious as she pulled the Suburban back onto the road again. She was oddly calm, but she didn't offer any information.

"What is it?" I finally asked.

She swallowed hard as she glanced in the rearview mirror; and then she began to speak, as the boys happily chattered in the backseats.

"The doctor said the MRI showed an abnormality. He wants to do an MRI spectroscopy to have a closer look at your brain tissue. It's a better MRI that'll show definitive details, and indicate whether it's *specifically* lymphoma. The doctor said the scan lights up like a Christmas tree if lymphoma is present. The abnormality might be nothing at all or it might..." Keri paused. "Or it might... or it might be lymphoma."

I watched from her right side as she swallowed hard and focused at the road ahead. I knew her well enough to know she fought back tears because the boys were in the car with us. They didn't know about all we'd been going through and we'd wanted to spare them the worries we'd had in the past. Children shouldn't have to know about awful things like cancer. Their childhood innocence shouldn't be touched by such dreadful realities.

The boys happily talked in the back, aggravating each other, as boys do, and joked around, while music played from the car's speakers. Keri touched her left cheek, as she cleared her throat, and then reached for my hand as she quietly drove on. I'd look back on that time and realize just how strong my wife, the mother of our boys, had really been on that day. But in that moment, I felt sort of numb and in a fog-like stupor, almost like I couldn't relate to Keri's emotions.

Later that evening, the boys were playing and I was asleep, as usual. Keri got a call from my doctor to check-in with her and finalize the details of the MRI spectroscopy, scheduled for the next day. As she answered her phone, she rushed outside and onto our front porch to find a quiet place where she could talk with the doctor. The boys had been used to "being quiet while Dad was on a business call," but this was entirely different. Besides, it had been months since I'd had been on a business call, so the boys weren't used to having to keep it down during a phone conversation.

"*Now* do you believe me, Doctor?" Keri asked, after briefly listening to the doctor. "I've been trying to tell you something's very wrong!"

"I do. Yes, I do. He definitely has a brain abnormality."

The doctor went on to let Keri know when my scan was scheduled and they went over a few more details. By this time, Keri felt qualified to have medical conversations with my doctors, based on what I'd been through and all she'd learned about cancer, various treatments, side effects and even mortality rates. It was nothing she'd ever wanted to know, and nothing she'd expected to ever touch her family, but these things had become a real part of our world. Keri steeled herself and continued the conversation.

Keri got me to the appointment for the MRI spectroscopy and we waited for the results. While I slept enough for a half-dozen people, Keri could barely sleep at all as she continued to go through the motions of handling the boys and our family's routines.

Every time her phone rang, Keri grabbed it, eager to hear the results. Her heart pounded like a jackhammer in her chest when the next day she recognized the doctor's phone number on her phone's screen. She walked outside as she answered the call.

Not even a minute later, the color all drained from her face as she held her stomach and shut her eyes. The doctor continued speaking as Keri tried to remain calm and just breathe.

"Okay, Doctor, so what's our plan?" she asked. "If the lymphoma is back, then what's our plan?"

"First, we'll need to drill a small hole in his head and do a biopsy to confirm that it's lymphoma."

"But you think it is," Keri said.

"Most likely, yes. And if it is lymphoma, then we'll do intense chemotherapy with bone marrow shots and a stem cell transplant," he answered, "But it'll be an intense schedule. Rob will have four rounds of chemo in the hospital, over a three-week period each time. Then he'll be home for a two week break between rounds. It'll be tough and very regimented."

Keri walked down our driveway as she contemplated what I was in for and how she'd tell me. By this point in time, I barely spoke at all, and if I did, my voice was only a weak, hoarse whisper; and Keri had to lean over and put her ear by my mouth in order to even hear me.

She mulled over the doctor's plan for me and summoned her courage to finally ask the biggest question for which she wasn't sure she wanted an answer.

"Doctor, is it... Is it *worth* it? I mean, is it worth putting him through all that?"

For Keri, it had felt like I'd already been gone for months. The real Rob, the man she'd married, hadn't been in our home for so long. Her partner and the father of her children had disappeared and had left a hollow shell that only physically resembled her husband. But Keri hadn't heard my laugh, shared jokes with me or felt like her husband was with her for such a long time. To her, it was as if I'd already gone

away and left her, and like she'd been mourning her lost husband for the last five months as she had stoically pushed onward with the demands of life.

"Oh, Keri," the doctor sighed. "I know what you're asking."

"Look, I've done all the research, Doctor. I know what he's up against. Please just level with me!" she begged. "What are his chances for recovery — for a *full* recovery?"

By this point Keri felt like the doctor was also a friend. She was sure he knew what she was going through, that he empathized with her and that she could trust him.

"Well, *if* the treatment works… *if* it works, he'll have one year, maybe two - *if* he's lucky."

Never before had that little two-letter word meant so much. Not in all her years, had Keri placed so much hope in the conjunction 'if' as she thought of our boys and our family. She finally broke down and sobbed and so did the doctor.

Keri tried to digest what she'd heard. "I've known Rob since I was eight years old! What do I do?"

She paced in our driveway and choked on her sobs as she tried to figure out what to do next. While she and I had always discussed things and made big decisions together, Keri was all alone and on her own by this point. It was a lot to take in, as she weighed the options and considered what my quality of life might be life and for what period of time.

Keri wanted to make the right decision for me, since I couldn't make it for myself. She didn't want to put me through the treatment for *her*, for the boys or for purely selfish reasons. It had to be the best decision for me, as an individual. Keri tried to separate her own emotions, rationally consider the options and just think clearly.

"Keri, listen to me," the doctor finally said, after a few moments. "Whether or not we treat this, isn't an option. Rob's too young and too strong *not* to treat it."

The doctor's positivity and his affirmative declaration were just what Keri needed to hear. His words gave her a renewed strength and helped her to refocus again.

"I need to talk to Rob's family. I'm not sure what to do. I'm not sure what's right, but I want to do what Rob would want."

"How about if I meet with all of you and we can discuss things?" he offered.

"Yes. Yes, thank you."

Keri hung up with the doctor and then walked toward our front yard and sat down in the grass to dial Cindy. She regurgitated all the things the doctor had told her, and then they both broke down and sobbed together. Not a lot of words were exchanged as my wife and my sister wept together. But it was one of those times when words weren't needed.

"We can all talk about it and help you with this," Cindy assured her when she could speak again.

After she finished talking to Cindy, Keri hung up and went inside again. The boys were still playing together, completely unaware of the monster that threatened to take away their father and the happy family life they'd always known. It broke Keri's heart to think of the boys without their father. She went upstairs and found me asleep, just as she'd expected. She climbed into bed next to me and put her head on my chest.

I cuddled her closer, without opening my eyes, as she began to speak in a soft, sad voice.

"It's in your brain, Rob. Lymphoma is in your brain."

I opened my eyes and looked down into hers that were wet with tears.

"Okay," I said with no real emotion, as if she'd just said something innocuous like I needed to change a light bulb or take out the trash.

What she'd said did register with me on some level. It meant I had something else to do and something else to worry about in my tired, foggy state.

"I need to get a job then," I added. "If something happens to me, I need to make sure you and the kids are okay."

I hadn't gotten over losing my job and being let go from Hydeswort. It had been a painful blow that had cut me to the core and made me question who I was as a man, a husband and a father. When I'd been a busy executive, I'd been in control of my world, responsible to many people and proud of my accomplishments. But when Hydeswort had pulled the rug from under my feet, I'd been left shaken and rattled, and I was no longer sure of how or where I fit into the world. The questions of 'Who am I?' often plagued me.

Keri and I lay together, quietly holding each other, and contemplating our scary and uncertain future. The sounds of our boys playing and laughing reminded me of my biggest worry:*What would happen to them and to Keri if I weren't around for them?* It was all so unfair — not just to me, but to all of us — and I was just too exhausted to deal with it, so I shut my eyes and fell asleep again.

10

Clinically Dead

By Chad Vangaalen

When I phoned my parents to tell them our latest bad news, it was Mom who answered. She listened quietly as I shared what Keri had learned from my doctor. Mom had always been strong, in control and not overly emotional in the face of situations. But I knew she got off the phone quickly so she could cry in private.

My parents and Keri's dad joined Keri and me at the University of Michigan to get a second opinion. Keri's mom watched the boys for us on that day. As always, I followed our little entourage, matching their steps and taking a seat when they did.

While I was physically in the room, it was again as if I weren't really there, an integral part of what went on around me. I was merely a passive observer. Everyone discussed *me*, asked questions and made the decisions for *me*, as I watched and listened, completely unable to participate in the exchanges.

The scene was a whole new dynamic for our marriage, since I had always been the one who did the planning for our family. But on that day, Keri jumped in and shouldered the burden at a time when I couldn't. I'd

look back later and realize she'd always been quite capable of handling things, but that I'd always felt the need to take care of things for our family.

The meeting that day yielded another option before jumping in and drilling into my brain. Dr. Junck, my doctor at the University of Michigan had a different take on things.

"Why drill?" Dr. Junck said. "There's a 99.9% likelihood that it's lymphoma. I think we need to skip the biopsy and just start treatment."

As Dr. Junck began his paperwork, my mom brought out some papers she'd brought from home.

"Doctor," Mom said, "This is some research I found online about a new way to treat lymphoma in the brain."

"Ahhhh, yes," Dr. Junck said as he looked at the research, "I actually worked on this."

The research documented in the article discussed a special cocktail of chemotherapy and medications that are easier on the body, but that still aggressively attack the cancer cells. It seems that the brain naturally protects itself, but Dr. Junck's methods allowed the medications to cross the natural barrier and get to the cancer cells.

"Our plan," Dr. Junck added, "Will be to treat Rob over four or five days, and then give him four to five weeks off, as opposed to Beaumont's plan that would put him in the hospital for three weeks at a time, and then out for two."

The conversation continued, and it sounded intelligent and thoughtful, as everyone seemed to be working together to come up with a plan for me. Again, it was a bizarre scene, as I sat, like a mute onlooker, while others discussed what would be best for me.

I heard all their words and I saw how serious everyone's demeanor was, but I couldn't really process the gravity of what they said. It

seemed like they were all a team though and all working toward the same goal as heads began to nod around me. In time, I silently filed out with my family, got in our car and went home again, so I could take a much needed nap.

I knew Keri talked to our family and friends, but she also wrote her thoughts in a journal as a way of coping:

Rob has been slowly leaving me, slipping away a bit at a time. How I wish he were here with me, juggling things and helping me to figure out what to do! It feels like I've been widowed for months now. He's physically here, right beside me; and yet I'm still so lonely without him.

I guess this is what it's like to be a single parent. What's so hard though is the overwhelming sadness and loneliness. It breaks my heart to not have my partner here to talk with and laugh with.

I'd do anything to have my husband back with me, but this time has also revealed a side of me that's given me a new sense of strength and independence too. Who knew I could repair things around the house? Who knew I could deal with our bills, budgeting and running our entire household? Who knew I'd be our family's primary caretaker?

It would be so nice to hear Rob's laughter again though, or to see his eyes light up - or even to have an argument with him! I miss him. I'm grateful to stay so busy or else I know I'd be swallowed whole by the overwhelming sadness.

As one day melded into the next, I heard the words that swirled all around me, but my brain couldn't respond to what I heard. Sometimes, when I heard conversations, I wanted to speak up and to participate, but the words just wouldn't come to my lips. The words were locked away somewhere deep inside and try as I might, I just couldn't bring them out!

It had been that way for six frustrating and exhaustive months. I'd felt trapped inside my own body, just existing, but not engaging with others and not really living. I was trapped in such a lonely place too, just as Keri was also in her own sad, lonely place, though I didn't know it then. We were right beside each other, and yet we couldn't connect anymore. For her though, it was much more difficult because she understood what was happening and she still had to take care of our boys, our family — and *me*.

I'll admit that during those days I thought about what it might be like to die. I had questions, although I couldn't talk to anyone about them. They were buried deep inside my head, locked away and far from ever escaping my lips because I couldn't form even simple sentences anymore.

The kids had gotten used to the fact that Dad slept all the time and Mom took care of them and ran the household. Dad was just *there*, breathing but emotionless, *existing* but not really *living* any sort of life. Keri struggled with explaining the situation to them. When the cancer was in

my sinus they knew "daddy's nose was sick". Now Keri told them "Daddy's brain is sick." I knew, in my heart, that I loved my wife and my children, but I could no longer express it to them. My heart knew it, but my brain wouldn't give me the words to tell them. I had no expression and no reaction, one way or another, to anything or anyone.

There was no joy, no laughter, no sadness and no fear. There was nothing. It felt as if my emotions had all been drained from my body. I felt hollow and empty, just a shell without any contents. Just the thought of trying to articulate my thoughts was exhausting. My family realized the cancer had affected the parts of my brain that controlled my speech; but all I knew was that I felt entirely disconnected from the world and everyone in it. It was as if the world moved on around me, but I couldn't keep up anymore. I couldn't engage with anyone or anything. While I'd once been able to juggle a dozen things at once, while also thinking about several more, I couldn't even grasp the simplest concepts anymore.

What is happening to me? I wondered from inside my lonely shell.

Keri continued to field phone calls, emails and texts from friends and family. She often resorted to texting to let people know what was going on:

Thank you all for keeping in touch. We feel comfortable with Dr. Junck at U of M and so we're moving ahead. There are multiple spots in Rob's brain that are affected. They're not actually attached though. They're like 'wisps' that freely 'float' around in the center of Rob's brain, making it impossible to go in and remove the cancer. We just hope and pray the treatment works. I'll keep you up to date on things. Thank you all for your continued prayers!

Keri and our families made the decision to move forward. Before starting treatment, Keri decided to throw a "Kicking Cancer Again" party. All of our close friends and family came over for Mexican food and margaritas. I sat at the kitchen counter, silently staring at the granite, while everyone I loved greeted me and wished me well. I barely reciprocated the conversation, just ate the food Keri put in front of me and sat silently. Thinking back, I barely remember this get together. I've been told that, for a lot of people who came, they were startled to see my sallow face and blank eyes. Emails and text updates didn't properly convey how serious the situation was. Many people left with tears in their eyes and continued crying on the drive home. The situation was grim and now everyone knew it firsthand.

My loved ones were all cautiously optimistic as my treatment began the next week. I was in the hospital for four days but, once again, I was never alone. Both Keri's parents and my parents rotated turns staying with our boys so Keri could be with me.

I thought of my boys and then I thought of my dad and the relationships I had with all of them. I imagined how hard it must have been for him, as my father, to watch what was happening to his son. Even in my altered state, I still knew how terrifying it would be for me if one of our boys had cancer. But just like always, Dad was optimistic and positive on the outside, as was everyone in our family.

The actual treatments took about four hours, as we waited, the chemo cocktail slowly dripped from the IV into my veins. It was strange to think about the medicine killing off the bad cancer cells, since it meant good cells would be destroyed too. But it didn't seem like I had any better options.

The whole process was very regimented and orderly, as each step was administered, one at a time. The day before a treatment, I received sodium

bicarbonate every four hours that protected my kidneys. On the first day of a three-hour chemo treatment, I also received anti-nausea meds and Benadryl. Then, on the next day, I got the Cytarabine, the rough meds that cross the blood/brain barrier to kill cancer cells by interfering with DNA synthesis. All this would be followed by constant saline flushes to clear out all the toxins.

The doctors and nurses had their routines, and Keri and I also created ours. She and I passed the time watching favorite TV shows like Breaking Bad. Keri lowered the AC thermostat in my room and brought our own blankets from home, so we got comfortable. On Tuesdays we spent the entire day watching the Law and Order SVU marathon. On Thursdays, the hospital cafeteria baked chocolate peanut butter bars; and Keri and I always split one. Every day at 3 o'clock Keri brought me a Starbucks Frappuccino. We had our little routines that we fell into, but no matter what, we kept our spirits high and we laughed. We *always* laughed together, which reminds me of the saying "Laughter is the best medicine!"

During my treatments, Keri also began online classes to renew her teaching certification. While I slept, she did her required reading – unless of course it was a Tuesday, when we watched Law & Order SVU. We always joked that it was impossible for Keri to study on those days.

We tried to keep things as normal as possible. To that end, my parents sometimes brought the boys to visit me at the hospital. We'd all walk down the hallways together as we talked and visited.

As Dr. Junck had explained, we did the chemo treatments in four-day intervals, went home for a few weeks; and then returned again for another IV cocktail, starting the process all over again. Since Keri and I had always loved movies, she and I made sort of a date out of the repetitive process and we went to a movie before my treatments started. The movies

provided a welcome respite from all that was going on. For a couple hours anyway, Keri and I could get away and feel normal again, even if only for a short while until the credits began to roll on the movie screen.

Keri's biggest fear was that the Rob she had known was gone forever and would never return to her. After the second round of chemo, she shared my progress in a text:

He's coming back! It's like a light switch has been flipped and I've started to see the old Rob again! He smiled this morning and made a sarcastic comment about his breakfast. It was amazing!

During my treatments, I'd sometimes have a problem with urine incontinency, possibly a result of the lymphoma disrupting messages to my brain. There were times when I'd have no warning whatsoever; and then all of a sudden, Keri would leap up and help me race into the bathroom. Occasionally, I didn't make it in time, so Keri started bringing spare clothes for me to the treatments. She soon learned where to find extra gowns and scrubs on the floor of the hospital too.

I found it was a good thing that my treatments were done at the hospital because the doctors were able to give me additional anti-nausea meds to help combat the nausea waves that came with the chemo. The meds helped so much. I only vomited during my first round of treatment, when we didn't yet realize nausea was going to be a problem.

Keri stayed by my side and she slept in a chair beside my bed that reclined and became a makeshift bed. It couldn't have been comfortable, but she did it; and I was comforted to have her beside me. The times when we were put in a private room, Keri could at least shower in the bathroom. But sometimes we shared a room with another patient, so that wasn't a possibility.

Our family and friends all pitched in to help us while Keri put all her energies into my treatments and communicating with my doctors. While I had hardly any strength, she seemed to have the strength of ten men. I marveled at all she did and all the while she had a positive attitude and a ready smile.

If the number of people who love a man determines his true wealth, then I must have been the wealthiest man alive. The continuous messages of encouragement and non-stop prayers meant so much to me, and sometimes they came at just the right time. Some were simple texts, others were phone calls or notes, but there was a constant stream of love and support and messages of:

Way to go, Rob! Kick cancer's butt!
Great news!
You're doing great! Get some rest!
We're praying for you, Rob! You've got this!

I don't think we realized just how many good friends and family members we had until this time. Besides all the calls, emails and texts, people went out of their way to make our lives easier. My mom and my cousin, Michele, along with two of Keri's friends, cleaned our entire house while Keri and I were away at the hospital. They even left fresh flowers for us. Keri's mom made sure the kids laundry was always washed and neatly put away. Keri's friends regularly took her out for "girl's nights" to check in and make sure she was handling everything ok. They were her rock; and they proved that 'family' doesn't only mean we share the same bloodlines.

My friends pitched in too, especially when they thought I might be depressed, before the lymphoma was diagnosed. Some took me to play golf, see Lions' games and watch movies. One friend went with me to buy a new bike. Another cleared my driveway every time it snowed. Even

when I was void of emotion, couldn't articulate my words and couldn't even keep my balance, these guys were there by my side.

Other friends tried to help by bringing me a new juicer and a recipe book full of healthy options for me to try. We received a collection of gift cards to various restaurants, so we could order out, instead of making dinner at times, which was a huge help for our busy household. Everyone tried to do something to help me, Keri or our family. It was like we had a whole team of people helping us, holding us up and supporting us during the darkest time.

While I rested one day, Keri talked to friends and family and replied to multiple text messages at once:

> *After round five of chemo, Rob developed an awful stomachache. We thought it was either chemo side effects or the flu. When he started vomiting blood on Sunday, we knew it was something else. I took him to the Beaumont ER and he was checked in. It was his gall bladder. After the surgeons removed it, they found that it had turned completely black. The surgeon said it was one of the top three worst gall bladders he's ever seen! My parents took the kids for the week so I could be with him while he was in the hospital. Michele, Cindy and Rob's parents waited with me during his surgery, for moral support. As always, we thank all of you for your prayers. We're back home now and Rob is resting. Round Six of chemo has been pushed back a couple weeks to give him time to recuperate a bit. I'll keep you all updated and thank you again for your calls and prayers.*

After Round Six of chemo, I was once again scheduled for radiation at Beaumont, although Dr. Junck had some reservations about me doing it. We trusted him, so we wanted to hear what he had to say.

"I'm not sure if we should do your radiation," the doctor told us. "There are some possible cognitive side effects. Let me look into it and give it some thought about how we should proceed."

Keri and I weren't thrilled about having my brain radiated, so we were glad the doctor wanted to look into it further. We trusted his opinion.

Before long, we all decided that I should go ahead and do the radiation, but that we'd do the minimum number of treatments and the minimum dosage of radiation. It was a full-head treatment, but each session lasted only three minutes. The radiation was harder on me this time though than it had been the previous time, and I ended up doing twelve out of a possible fifteen sessions.

On my last day of radiation, since we'd previously learned of the significance of the 'bell ceremony,' all of our family came to watch me ring the bell and celebrate the end of my treatment. Keri and the boys were there, as well as my parents, Keri's parents, my sister and my brother-in-law. Afterwards, we all went out to brunch together. By this time, I felt completely exhausted and my energy had been entirely sapped as if the life had been drained from my body. I was worn out again and just wanted to get home and rest.

During the three weeks following my final radiation treatment, I was so weak and so tired that I really thought I might actually die. I had zero energy, I couldn't articulate words that were in my head and it felt like I still couldn't relate to my old world. Keri constantly helped me, doing things for me, bringing me water or more blankets. Even the simple task of daily showers was completely exhaustive. I'd be in the shower for an hour as the water ran over me, but I was too weak to shampoo myself. Keri even had to help me to put on my socks and underwear.

My skin looked like a crude colorful mosaic of peeling skin, all in various stages of healing. The itchiness was excruciating. I could hardly stand it. I felt like I wanted to itch myself from the inside out. While I didn't like how I *looked*, my outward appearance still wasn't nearly as awful as I *felt inside*. Exhaustion was an understatement.

It was during this time that I couldn't even verbalize the name of our oldest son. He's my dad's namesake and his middle name is also Keri's father's name. The only thing worse than the total exhaustion and constant fatigue was the frightening frustration that also plagued me.

"I can't do this anymore," I told Keri one day. "It's like I beat the cancer with chemo, but now the radiation is going to take me out."

"You'll get past it," Keri reassured me. "You will. Just get through one day at a time."

GO! GO! GO! I silently reminded myself.

Just when I thought I could take no more, I began to feel just the slightest bit better. It was also nearly time for me to go back and see Dr. Junck for a follow-up visit.

11

Rise

By Calla

Keri drove me to my appointment with Dr. Junck. First though, the doctor had scheduled me for an MRI, so I went to Radiology before we saw the doctor. I used to be claustrophobic, but after so many MRIs, I trained myself to forget the anxiety I felt in small spaces. I listened to music and cleared my mind while the noisy machine went to work. After the MRI was done, Keri and I met with Dr. Junck an hour or so later.

"Rob, I want to do a few simple memory tests with you," the doctor explained. "Just basic stuff to check cognitive and balance reactions."

"Okay, sure."

"I'd like you to remember these three words: *Ohio, cat, shoe,*" he said.

"Okay, sure. No problem," I said.

Dr. Junck then went on to talk about other general things, like the weather and our boys. The atmosphere was light and he and I talked briefly.

"Now, Rob," the doctor said, about five minutes later, "What were those three words I asked you to remember?"

The words... the three words....What were they?

My mind raced and searched to recall those three simple words. It had only been a few minutes since he'd told me to remember them.

I glanced at Keri, seated beside me, as she bit her bottom lip, looked at me and silently willed me to recall the three simple words.

Surely I can recall something so simple!

I wracked my brain and quickly became frustrated. It was as if I could *see* the words, even *spell* the words; but I couldn't *articulate* them!

"I can't!" I blurted out as my palms sweat and my heart raced. "I can't recall the words!"

Keri put her hand on my arm to reassure me.

"It's alright, Rob," Dr. Junck said. "It's early still. Give it some time. Sometimes it takes a little longer for the neural cognitive impairments to repair themselves. Let's move on to a few other tests."

He asked me to walk up and down the hall while he watched and made notes. I couldn't keep my balance and I was unable to walk in a straight line. The doctor intently watched and he made notes. Then he asked me to balance on just the balls of my feet and then to squat with my hands held out in front of me. It was obvious to all of us that my ability to keep my balance had been affected. The doctor made more notes, and then he tested the strength of my handgrip and my pull-push abilities. I was unable to push back against his hands and most notably I couldn't make my hands roll as the doctor had asked. It was awkward and frightening to not be able to do the simple tasks as directed.

"Good. Okay, that's good," Dr. Junck said automatically as he wrote on his chart. "I'd like for you to start speech therapy and physical therapy, Rob. We'll get it set up for you and someone will call you about the dates. Speech therapy will help you with your memory recall and with physical therapy, you'll begin to see improvements, little by little, in your balance and flexibility."

Keri had been raised in a Catholic home and our boys were Catholic. I'd considered converting to Catholicism before, but more than ever, I felt like I needed something more to hang onto at this time in my life. I needed to have the strength of something bigger than myself, something omnipotent that could bear some of the burden of all I was feeling.

It was August 2014 when I began the process of converting to Catholicism. I also started physical therapy around the same time. It felt right to me that I should work on my physical self, as well as my spiritual self, at the same time. Renewing and revitalizing my whole self became my mission, and I delved into the process full-force, just as I'd have taken on a project at work. I did research, read, made plans, set goals and measured and recorded my progress. 'Rebuilding Rob' became my job and I was determined to come back better and stronger than before cancer had interrupted my life and upended my whole family's world.

Physical therapy was sometimes difficult, but even the worst days were made better by the wonderful people at the therapy offices. The therapists helped me improve my balance and work on my flexibility. We worked toward having me walk more erect; and in time, we corrected the shuffling that had become my signature gait; but my shoulder still continued to droop. It took about six months for me to relearn many simple, basic things I'd done without even thinking for four decades. It was truly humbling, at times, to realize I was working on things so simple, and things I'd taken for granted my whole life.

My physical therapy was made more difficult by the fact that I'd gotten out of shape in the last year when I'd been solely concentrating on battling cancer. I was overweight by this time, but I was also bloated due to all the steroids I'd been taking. I wasn't happy with my appearance and I knew getting in shape would make me feel better, both physically and mentally.

My therapists, Heather and Karen, were sensitive to my physical state, as they helped me work at my own pace until I finally built up some endurance and strength again. Their positive attitudes, compassion and genuine friendliness pulled me through some really rough times. They weren't there to only work on my physical needs, but rather they took into consideration 'my whole being' while they worked with me.

On those occasions when I felt exhausted and like giving up, I silently reminded myself to *'Go! Go! Go!'* as I repeatedly vowed to *kick cancer's ass*. Those simple words, *'Go! Go! Go!'* became my trademark mantra, and before long, even the therapists were repeating them too.

"Come on, Rob!" they'd cheer. "Go! Go! Go! Two more reps!" Or "Go! Go! Go! You've got this, Rob!" And "One more lap, Rob! *Go! Go! Go!*"

In addition to the physical therapists, I also had a trainer at my gym who helped me to learn the various machines and how to use them correctly for optimum results. As I got stronger physically, and fed my soul spiritually, I felt myself evolving and growing.

It was like my life was divided into two segments: my first life, *before* cancer, and my second life, *after* cancer. My 'first life,' in the fast-paced corporate world, had been one of pressures, deadlines, projects, and endless workdays that merged one into the next. In my first life, I worked diligently to provide *for* my family, but I was so overworked that I didn't get to be *with* my family. I largely contributed to the big picture, but I never had time for the details or the little moments that *made up* that marvelous big picture — and our boys were growing up fast.

In my 'second life' though, my world had slowed down, whether I'd wanted it to or not. I was no longer on the outside, looking in, and just seeing the big picture. I was *inside* the big picture, an integral and hands-on part of it, as I navigated the intricacies of our family life. With Keri back to work, I'd begun to help with some of the parenting duties for our

family. Keri still got the boys ready for school in the mornings, did the laundry and cooked dinner; but I took them to the bus stop and drove them to their practices to help as much as I could. I'll admit that it felt good when it was sometimes *Dad* whom the boys called for when they fell off a skateboard, needed help with their homework or required a referee. It felt good to once in a while have them rely on me and reach out for me, instead of only viewing me as the 'busy parent whose cell phone was eternally attached to his head.'

"You know, " I told Keri one night. "I had no idea what I was missing out on for all those years."

"And the boys really like having you at home too," she agreed. "You're getting to know them on another level. You'd have missed out on so much. It's like the silver lining in what you've been through in the last couple years."

Keri and I had lots of talks when I was able to speak again, and I made sure she knew how much she'd contributed to my positive outcome. She was my rock who held me up, both figuratively, and many times even literally. I think we both learned something about ourselves, as well as each other, during the darkest time of our lives. What I learned was that I couldn't have found a better wife than Keri, and our boys couldn't have a better mother. Not only did she bear an immense burden and take charge of our whole life, but she also became my advocate, making some difficult decisions when I wasn't able. There were many times when I reflected on our marriage vows of "for better or for worse and in sickness or in health," and realized the intensity and depth of our promises to one another.

As I continued with my Catholic conversion, I prayed more and I repeatedly thanked God for all the good things I had in my life. I may have been working hard to recover from what my body had been put through, but I felt like one of the luckiest and most blessed guys on Earth!

12

Alive & Amplified

By The Mooney Suski

My 'second life,' as I like to refer to it, meant that I had to learn some things – a lot of things really. In my 'first life,' I was always the guy who arrived home after dark to a nicely manicured lawn, but it was because I'd hired a lawn service, since I never had time to care for it myself. Today, Max handles that responsibility and happily mows it with his new riding mower.

When Keri and I were first married, the only thing I knew how to cook was anything from a can that was marked *Chef Boyardee*. I'll never cook like Keri, and I think we're all happier to leave most of the cooking to her, but my mom has been teaching me to cook a few things. While I used to be a great delegator, today I try to be more participative and hands-on with things. Keri and I have worked out systems that work for both of us, and that work for our family, again representative of the 'give and take' that's found in marriages.

I've always been a huge music fan and over the last 28 years, I've been to more concerts than I can even count. Music has always been very important to me and I've got the biggest CD collection of anyone I've met, with thousands neatly lining the wall shelves in my home office. Keri and I usually only went to concerts in the Detroit area because of my work schedule, but since I wasn't working, we had more flexibility.

"This will be the Year of the Concerts!" I proclaimed in early 2014.

Keri and I went to concerts in four states that year – Michigan, Ohio, Illinois and Nevada. We went to a three-day music festival in Chicago with friends. We flew to Las Vegas to see one of our favorite bands, Jane's Addiction. We drove to Cleveland to see the Rock & Roll Hall of Fame and attend a concert; and then, the next day, we drove to Columbus to see another show.

I was still a bit weak, and couldn't stand for long periods of time, so Keri and I got seats in the venues' handicapped areas. But even this was a plus, because we were much closer to the stages. Again, there was a silver lining.

We'd decided to have as many adventures as possible and to live life to the fullest. We took the kids to Myrtle Beach; took two trips to Las Vegas – one to renew our wedding vows; went to Mackinac Island with my in-laws, Tom and Jackie; took the kids to Chicago and spent a month at Lake of the Ozarks. Every day was a blessing and gift, and we were determined to get as much out of life as possible.

After I'd survived my second bout with cancer, everything seemed more meaningful and important. The sky seemed bluer, flowers smelled sweeter and my wife's smile seemed broader. I'd always appreciated our families, but after the last couple years, they meant even more to me. Dad

and I had never missed a Detroit Lions game since 1996, no matter how sick I'd been, and I looked forward to carrying on the father-son tradition with each of my boys. Even the simplest things held deeper meaning and I was grateful for each one.

As much as I loved being part of the boys' lives on a more intimate level, it still bothered me that I wasn't fulfilling my traditional role as our family's main provider. In time, as I got stronger, I put out some feelers and looked into finding a job again.

At almost 43, and having been out of the workforce for a while, I found that getting a new job might not be as easy as it once had been. It was psychologically damning to me to be considered for positions that were well below the level I'd attained in my 'first life.' When I was let go from Hydeswort, there were only a handful of executives that had risen to the same level as I; and I knew that major retailers usually only have four employees at that level within their organizations, so my odds of landing a similar position weren't good.

It was a whole different world than the one I'd left where I'd been sought out and offered positions based on my reputation and previous performance in the industry. I liked that guy, whose reputation pre-ceded him, and whose work ethic was well known. It's who I was and it was my professional identity that told me how and where I fit into the world. In my 'second life,' I felt like a puzzle piece trying to find where I fit. The whole business of looking for a job was entirely new to me.

Just before Hydeswort had let me go, I'd brought on a new employee named Belinda. Imagine my surprise when I learned that as soon as they'd

fired me, Hydeswort gave my job to Belinda. Of course, I spent the next couple years feeling as if she and I were adversaries of a sort.

Belinda eventually was also let go by Hydeswort, a year after they fired me, and became a representative for a company based in Fort Wayne, IN. By the time our paths crossed again, she was the executive VP of Business Development for IDS.

"Rob!" Belinda said, "I've wondered how you've been doing!"

Her attitude was so positive and her voice so friendly. It perplexed me since I thought she'd essentially taken my job at Hydeswort. But as we talked, I realized that things were not at all as they'd seemed.

"I thought I'd be working with *you* when Hydeswort hired me," Belinda told me. "I was really mad and totally shocked when they let you go. No one saw it coming!"

I'd spent the past couple years having bad feelings for no reason at all. Things weren't as I'd imagined, and I'd wasted my time and energy dwelling on something that wasn't at all as I'd thought.

After we'd talked a few times, Belinda hired me as VP of Business Development, the same position I'd held at Hydeswort. And better still was the fact that I could work from my home office in my new position. If things hadn't all fallen into place as they did, I'd never have had the opportunity to work with such a quality person in such a great organization. Things happen for a reason.

With my health improving and my new job, things were definitely looking up. But something had been bothering me for well over a year. It was the thing that kept me up some nights and the one thing that occupied my mind as unfinished business. I hadn't resolved things with Bruce at

Hydeswort, and I've never been the kind of guy to leave things undone. I had to have resolution with how I'd been treated and what had been done to me. The fact that Hydeswort had settled out of court with me was a sort of resolution in itself but what I needed was more of a personal conclusion. It was just something I had to do in order to once and for all close the final chapter on my 'first life.'

After considering what I wanted to say to Bruce, I phoned him one afternoon. Because I was still having some memory issues and difficulty recalling how to say certain words, I wanted to stay focused and to get right to the point of my call.

"Rob Atteberry!" Bruce said when he took my call. "How are you doing?"

"I need to talk to you, Bruce."

"Okay, sure. Come on down to the office."

I went to the corporate offices and was buzzed into the second floor where Bruce's office is located.

"I'll get Bruce for you," the receptionist told me.

Moments later, Bruce came out of the boardroom and we shook hands and exchanged pleasantries.

"We can step in here," Bruce said and I followed him back into the boardroom.

After we sat down, I looked him in the eye and said, "Bruce, I am going to talk to you. I do not want you to talk. This is what I am here to tell you: I came to work here, back in 2012, because you were my mentor and I wanted to work for you again. I was doing well, but then I got cancer, and you let me go. That was a problem. I put off my radiation treatments because I thought I no longer had insurance. My cancer ended up coming back in my brain. It's a long and intense story, but thanks to my family and friends, I got through it. Little by little, I grew

stronger, learned to walk and talk again and be a husband and a father again. But through it all, I wondered how to explain to my kids that their father had no job. I am here today to tell you to look in the mirror, Bruce; and don't ever repeat what you did to me. Don't put someone else through the hell that you put me through. And by the way, I'm in remission now."

Bruce didn't look at me for much of what I said to him. He looked down and hung his head slightly as I spoke. I wondered if he'd expected to hear from me, and maybe even if he felt he deserved to be admonished like a child.

When I'd finished speaking, Bruce took a deep breath and looked up.

"Congratulations," he said, almost robotically and automatically.

"Thank you," I calmly said. "I'm going to leave now."

I got up and walked out of the boardroom and through the door. As I walked through the lobby, I felt a little bit lighter.

"Hey, Rob!" Bruce called behind me. "Rob, wait a minute."

I turned around, as Bruce walked up to me.

"You know Bruce, I was a vice-president for you at Gechsmin; I was a vice-president at Tendlart; and then a vice-president for you *again*, at Hydeswort. You could've put me on disability; but you fired me. Things could have been different and so much easier," I said.

"I know," was all Bruce said.

Shaking my head, I turned my back on Bruce; but this time, I kept walking. I wondered if Bruce had so little to say because the Legal Department had told him not to discuss the matter with me or anyone else. Nonetheless, I felt great when I walked out of the building on that day. As the door closed behind me, I knew I had also closed the final chapter on my 'first life' and I felt satisfied.

That night, I easily fell asleep and slept better than I had in the longest time. When the sun came up the next morning, it brought with it the promise of good things in my 'second life,' and I was ready to embrace all of them.

13

True Faith

By New Order

While life had started looking up for me, I realized I was growing and becoming a different person in a lot of ways. I looked at life differently and I valued my life and the persons in it even more. Instead of being constantly distracted and having a cell phone plastered to my ear all the time, I embraced everyone and everything in my life, and I thanked God for all the blessings around me, big and small. Instead of being distracted and in a hurry all the time, I slowed down to enjoy the little things like stealing a kiss from my wife at a stoplight or getting caught in the rain while we were out for a walk. Instead of being irritated that the dog's toys were on the floor, I was grateful that I could walk over and pick them up. Instead of immediately becoming stressed over situations, I reminded myself how awesome it is to *be here* to deal with those situations. I just saw things differently and in a new light. Compared to what I'd been through, life looked pretty good to me.

It was spring 2015, and I was nearing the end of my conversion to Catholicism. (Coincidentally, my Cobra insurance coverage was nearing

its end too.) During a six-hour Sabbatical with Father Mike in March, he related a story to me. He told me of a 27-year-old, good-looking guy who had a million dollars and found out he had cancer.

"So what did he do?" I asked.

"Well, he took all his money and he went to Florida," Father Mike said.

"And?"

"*And he died.* He didn't ask for God's help; he didn't seek guidance; and he didn't try to save himself. Instead, he died with a full bank account and an empty heart."

"You know, Father Mike, I had cancer before," I confided, "But now I'm in remission. It was a combination of things — family, friends, fitness, the doctors — that helped, but I know God is the reason I'm still here."

"Well, I'm certain of it," Father Mike agreed.

When my 30-month Cobra coverage ended on March 31, 2015, I was forced to go on Medicare. Keri and the boys are today covered under ObamaCare. I really resented, as I still resent today, that Hydeswort never gave me the opportunity to go on disability. They instead chose to permanently sever my employment and effectively throw my world, and my family's world, into a tailspin. Life was made so much more difficult as a result; and the stress was compounded tenfold because of the company's irresponsible decisions and inhumane actions.

A few days before my Cobra coverage ended, I sat down in front of my computer and opened my Facebook page. There were the usual new postings, and then I saw a familiar name in the comments section under the recent update I'd posted about my good MRI scan.

Steve Ryman had been my indirect boss years before when I'd been with Gechsmin. Seeing his name reminded me of the great guy Steve was and how he'd been so supportive during my cancer battle.

"Freaking fantastic news about your PET scan!" he wrote on March 27. "You've *got* to write a book! Now get going on it! You'll make a million dollars!"

I laughed aloud at Steve's comment, 'liked' it and went on to read other Facebook posts.

Just five days later, I got some devastating news: Steve had committed suicide. As I talked with people, it became clear that due to his own medical problems and his dismal prognosis, Steve had decided when and how he'd leave this life on his own terms. He had lost his sight in one eye and was rapidly losing sight in his other eye. Steve had never married and he had no kids; and so I presumed he just didn't want to live without his sight.

When I heard the awful news, I went to Steve's Facebook page and immediately saw the familiar photos of Steve with his beloved horses and dogs. Everyone who knew Steve also knew how much he'd loved animals. Steve was that person who gave of himself and always helped others. He'd been such a great guy, loved and respected by so many. And just as he'd always been in charge of his life, Steve also made the decision, at age 59, to check out on his own terms and in his own time. He'd even left instructions that he wanted no funeral or service of any kind.

It seemed bizarre to me that I was fighting with everything I had, to live and to stay here with Keri and our boys, but that Steve had chosen to leave this world. I reasoned though that he must have made the best decision for himself and his circumstances, just as I'd done too. I prayed for Steve and I even talked to him, and I told him we'd meet again one day — but not too soon, if I had anything to say about it.

Following Steve's death, I vowed to lead a full and valuable life. I realized that even in death, Steve continued to be an inspiration to me; and it was his final Facebook message to me that ultimately prompted me to share my own journey with others.

Just a few days later, on Easter Sunday, I completed my conversion to Catholicism. That day held special meaning for me as I embraced not only my 'second life,' but also my deeper relationship with God. I was new, healthy and whole that day, and I was so grateful to still be here with my family.

As great as life looked for me, I was also aware that many others still suffered with cancer and the collateral damage it left. I'd become active in Gilda's Club, both for myself and also to help other cancer patients and their families.

The original chapter of Gilda's Club was formed in New York and named for Gilda Radner, the brilliant comedian and an original cast member of Saturday Night Live. Even after Gilda was diagnosed with ovarian cancer in 1986, she continued to make people laugh, as she learned to live with her cancer. It had always been her dream that all persons touched by cancer would be able to receive the social and emotional support she'd found during her battle. After she lost her battle in 1989, her husband Gene Wilder and her cancer psychotherapist formed the first Gilda's Club. Six years later, the New York City chapter officially opened its doors and the members poured in through the group's signature red door, which represents Gilda's legacy to those living with cancer.

Gilda's Club is intended to be a gathering place where cancer patients and their families go to find social and emotional support as a supplement to medical care. With nearly 15,000,000 people diagnosed with cancer each year, many people rely on their Gilda's Club meetings and look forward to passing through the red door and finding understanding, solace and hope on the other side.

Since I'd beaten cancer twice, I resolved to be a beacon of hope for people who were in the battle of their lives and for their very lives. My involvement with Gilda's Club led me to meet some incredible people, but one thing that I found eye-opening is the fact that a lot of cancer patients don't have as much support as I'd had during my own cancer fights. Many cancer patients couldn't afford the chemotherapy recommended by their doctors, and so their visits to Gilda's Club were the only medicine they received.

We all had different stories, various circumstances and other things that separated us; and yet the one thing we shared was our battle with cancer. I really made an effort to connect with people and to offer them hope at these groups. Attending the meetings was very intense and emotionally draining. I'd even continue to feel exhausted through the following day. But since I'd beaten cancer not once, but twice, I owed it to others to be a living example of someone who had made it out the other side and defeated the monster that they all battled.

In addition to sharing our health issues and our personal experiences with our cancers, the members in our group also shared personal problems and even stories of our own insurance woes. It was obvious that while we all shared some similarities, we also had different dynamics at play in our personal lives too. For me, my health had become a top priority, so I decided to focus on a goal of preparing for an upcoming triathlon as a way to stay focused.

With everything going on in 2014, it was important to me that I had a goal, something to work toward, a deadline of sorts that would measure my progress. Maybe that mindset was formed during my days in the corporate world, but I'm a guy who enjoys that sort of thing, even thrives in that atmosphere. It was for this reason, that I was determined to complete the September 2014 Reeds Lake Triathlon.

In 2009, the Reeds Lake Tri was the first one in which I'd ever competed. Years later, with all I'd been through, I wanted to do it again; and prove to myself that I was indeed 'back.' To train for the 2014 tri, I ran, biked and swam, in an attempt to prepare my body for the half-mile swim, 18.5-mile bike ride and four-mile run.

Just a couple months after I'd completed speech and physical therapy, I was back at the Reeds Lake Tri with about 1200 other athletes, each of whom were there for their own reasons too. For years, the tri had been held to promote an active, healthy lifestyle; and to raise awareness for the Mary Free Bed Rehabilitation Hospital Foundation and to restore hope and freedom through rehabilitation. Similarly, I was there after I'd also found hope and freedom through rehab too; but I was also there to prove something to myself and to cap-off the progress I'd made in recent months.

On this day, even Keri had prepared and trained to compete in the team relay event. She was her team's swimmer for the first part of the tri; Jill was the cyclist; and Theresa was the runner. Our friend, Shannon, had organized two other relays of women, all wearing *Team Atts* shirts.

The air was blanketed with a team spirit on one of the most perfect Michigan days we'd had in a while, almost as if God smiled down and rejoiced with us in my triumph over cancer. The skies were blue and clear, and the temperature was about 70-degrees. Wet suits were needed for the swimmers, but the temperature was perfect for the cyclists and runners.

While I'd had the support of all our family and friends, right from the beginning of my battle with cancer, it was still amazing to see all of them who'd come out to support me on that day. There was an endless sea of blue T-shirts, emblazoned with *Team Atts* on the fronts and *Go! Go! Go!* on the backs. The presence of *Team Atts* energized me; and the air was charged with the love and encouragement of people who mean the most to me. No matter my official time that day, I already felt like a winner before I even started.

From the moment I took my first stroke in the lake's frigid water, our friend, James, was by my side; and he never left me, as he matched his strokes to mine. His presence pushed me, stroke after stroke, as I cut through the water. When I got to the other side of the lake, I ran from the water's edge to pick-up my bike; and Bob and James were right there too. I was empowered by my friends' support, as I pedaled for all I was worth, and left cancer behind, in my past.

This is what life's all about! I thought. *This is what's important!*

Just seven months before, I'd completed my radiation treatments and had then begun speech and physical therapy. The road hadn't been easy, but it was made much easier by family and friends like those on the bikes beside me. As I focused on the road in front of me, I pedaled into my future, excited for what would come next.

When I came to the end of the 18.5-mile route, I dropped my bike and instantly began the final leg, the four-mile run. Bob and James were still right there with me; and Theresa ran with us too at this point, doing her part of the relay for Keri's team. I maintained a run-walk pace, by this point; but our friends still stayed beside me and kept pace with me, ignoring their own potential and finish times.

About a mile from the finish line, another friend, Marc, ran up and joined our group. Marc had already completed the course, but he'd come back to run with me and encourage me as I headed for the finish line. As I

focused and controlled my breathing, step after step, I felt the support of my friends, as sure as if they'd carried me and lifted me up. They all knew though how important it was for me to get to the end of the race, unassisted and on my own. They knew what it meant to me.

"You've got this, Rob!" they said. "Almost there! You're doing great!"

Finally, the finish line came into view, roped-off with yellow tape and surrounded by orange cones and tents on either side. But it wasn't the finish line that I focused on as I made my way to the end of the race. It was the huge sea of blue T-shirts and homemade poster board signs made by *Team Atts.*

"Yeah, Dad! Come on, Dad!" my boys yelled from the sidelines, among the blue shirts that rose up around them.

My own sleeveless blue shirt got closer to the vast sea of blue, step-by-step, until I finally crossed the finish line. With tears in my eyes, hidden by my sunglasses, I crossed the white line with hands held high, as my friends hung back and allowed me to cross alone. It was the first time in two hours that they'd left my side. Enveloped by 60 blue shirts that wrapped me with their love, I was reminded of how and why I'm still here, and how grateful I am for this gift called Life.

The applause and cheers had made my finish seem more like a major sporting event, and I'd never felt better! As weak and lifeless as I'd been, just months earlier, in that moment, I felt invincible - like I could even move mountains! Friends and family cheered, clapped and took photos as Keri came to kiss me. She was right there just as she'd been from the very start of my cancer battle, to support me, hold me and lift me up.

The announcer told the crowd, "Well, I'll tell you one thing — this is the biggest cheering crew around! This is Mr. Rob Atteberry, folks! He's a Grand Rapids cancer survivor!"

Yes, I am! I thought. *I surely AM!*

No race had ever felt better and no finish line had looked brighter than the one on that important day. All our friends and family joined us for a great after-party at Marc and Shannon's house. We didn't just celebrate my completion of the tri though; we celebrated our love and friendship that day – the things that really matter.

"I want to thank each and every one you," I said, in a toast, as I looked at all the faces around me, "For being so important to my family and to me and for all you do for us. Everything about the tri was important, but what's more important is *all of you* and what you mean to our family and to me. Your love and support got us through one of the roughest times in our lives. I love all of you more than I can ever say. *Go! Go! Go!*"

After completing the triathlon in September 2014, it was still important to me to continue to get healthier and to continue to set goals for myself. When I'd first started competing in triathlons, it was because I'd put on some weight and I just wanted to get in shape again. But after beating cancer, the triathlons represented so much more than that to me. Training, competing and finishing triathlons allows me to set goals, work toward them and then compete, which allows me to see my efforts pay off. Charting and measuring my progress and my accomplishments is a visual reminder to me of how far I've come and the work I've done. Finishing a race or a triathlon doesn't just mean crossing the finish line. It means weeks and months of training have and culminated to prove that I'm transforming myself and getting stronger, that I'm healthy and that I'm still here!

14

Hands Up, Robert

By Saint Motel

With life looking up, and a few triathlons under my belt, my next goal was to complete the Muncie ½ Ironman in Muncie, Indiana in July 2015. I'd trained religiously, paced myself, set small and then larger goals, and kept my eye on my objective. I felt great, both physically and mentally, the week of the race.

But there was another equally important event on my calendar that same week. As eager as I was to complete in Muncie, I was also eager to have the MRI done that my doctor had scheduled for that same week.

The mood around our home was light and fun; and we were all in a great mood as the day of the race approached. During church on Sunday, I thanked God for all He'd done for me that had brought me to that week. I worked at home on Monday and met with a buyer in Grand Rapids on Tuesday. Keri and I cheered the boys on during a swim meet on Wednesday and then dropped all of them off at Keri's parents' home, so she and I could go to Detroit and see a Morrissey concert that night. The week had been fast-paced and it felt great to have a diverse, busy schedule and a typical family life once again.

"You know," I said to Keri as we drove to Detroit, "THIS is how it's supposed to be. THIS is how life should be."

She just smiled and held my hand tighter.

We had great seats for the concert that night. I'm not sure if it was because I was in a terrific mood or if it was simply because things looked, smelled and sounded more intense and with a fine-tuned clarity, but Morrissey was fantastic! It felt so good to have Keri by my side, as we enjoyed the concert together, free of the worry and the burden we'd shared. Just as she'd been beside me every step of the way during my journey through cancer, Keri was right there holding my hand that night and reminding me of what's really important in this life.

When the concert ended, we went to a hotel in Ann Arbor to get some sleep since my MRI was scheduled for 6 a.m. the next morning. Just as I'd done all week, I easily woke before our 4 a.m. alarm even sounded. I was ready to have the MRI done and get confirmation that the scan was good once again and still showed no changes.

When we arrived at the University of Michigan's cancer center, I felt good and I wasn't the least bit worried that we'd hear bad news after the MRI was completed. Keri and I thought only positive thoughts and we went in there merely as a formality, because we just knew I was going to be okay.

While completely still inside the MRI machine, I silently reminded myself, *'Go! Go! Go!'* The magnetic field and pulses of radio wave energy reverberated around my head as I lay perfectly still, just as I'd done for the previous three MRI scans, which had all yielded favorable results. I waited silently for the test to end that could detect tissue damage, signs of infection,

inflammation or cancer disease, although I was sure my results would be favorable.

Several hours later, Keri and I met with Jessica, Dr. Junck's Physician's Assistant. We were genuinely glad to see Jessica, because she had taken time off to have her baby before my treatments had ended. As we talked with her about her new baby, I was reminded that life goes on and that God is good indeed.

"Well, it's good news!" Jessica happily told us. "Everything looks good! No changes!"

Keri and I both breathed a sigh of relief. By this time, she and I were far beyond any sort of tears, either good or bad. We felt nothing but grate-fulness, thankfulness and sheer happiness on that morning! When Keri and I left Jessica, we hugged her and thanked her, grateful for another friend we'd made along our journey. We walked outside the University of Michigan's hospital doors and I was certain that the morning sun was shin-ing brighter than ever before and that God smiled down on us.

Great news everyone! Keri texted. *Rob's MRI results were good!*

I shared my latest good news on Facebook: MRI WAS GOOD!!! NO CHANGES!!! *GO! GO! GO!*

We drove home and then while Keri went to pick up Max and Wes from their tennis matches, I drove over to Keri's parents' home to pickup Zac and Ben. It felt great to be doing the simple 'Dad duties' that I might have missed out on if things had turned out differently. I knew I wouldn't still be here if I didn't have such a persistent wife who had fought for doc-tors to look harder and delve deeper only months before. We were eager to set out on our trip; and I couldn't wait to celebrate life when I com-pleted the Muncie ½-Ironman.

The next morning, Friday, we piled all the boys into our Suburban and our whole family set off for the four-hour drive to Muncie. Like on

all family car trips, the boys were buckled in back with all their important travel necessities, including videos, iPads, music, books, games and snacks.

As I drove along, it felt great to listen to the boys joking and playing in the backseat as Keri sat beside me. When I'd been a busy, successful executive, I'd thought I had it all, but I was now certain that I'd been very wrong. On this day, as I looked next to me and then into my rearview mirror, I realized that *now* I have it all!

We got up early on Saturday morning and I was eager to head over to the Prairie Creek Reservoir, located on more than 750 acres and about five miles southeast of Muncie. After 141 days of training, I felt ready to take on the challenge of the 70.3 miles that awaited me.

My cheering section was ready too, all wearing their familiar blue shirts that read *'Go! Go! Go!'* My parents, my sister, Cindy and her kids, and some family friends had all come to support me and to wait while I competed in all three events. My longtime friend, James, was there too. He had signed up to compete alongside me and make sure I made it through the race safely.

Of the 2,000 people who signed up, 1,760 participants competed that day. There were men and women of all different shapes, sizes and ages. There were even some handicapped participants too.

Keri and our kids sat by the water's edge and watched as I joined the other competitors in the first event, a 1.2-mile swim across a lake. Hands and feet rhythmically sliced through the water all around me as I swam hard and remained focused. It was reassuring to see James swimming alongside of me.

Go! Go! Go! I reminded myself. *Go! Go! Go!*

I'd trained in a swimming pool, but I still did well in the open water. I finished the swim in 40 minutes to place 100th out of 300 competitors in

my age group —not bad for a guy who couldn't even stand without toppling over just a year before!

I hurriedly got out of the lake and ran to the next event, the 55-mile bike ride. My body felt great. The endorphins pulsed through me as I concentrated on the road in front of me and paced myself. I wasn't hurting at all. In fact, I felt entirely exhilarated in the moment, as James and I raced my bike through rural Indiana. I knew the upcoming run would be tough, but I put the thought out of my mind and focused only on the task at hand as I concentrated on the road in front of me.

Go! Go! Go!

After I'd finished Mile 56, I dropped my bike and immediately began the 13.1-mile run around the south side of the reservoir, over rolling country roads and then back again. As I ran, I was so grateful to my Oakhurst Wolfpack running buddies who had faithfully trained with me in all kinds of weather. Come rain or come shine, and in all kinds of temperatures, they'd been there for me every day. I'd expected that the run would be tough, especially after the first two events, but I knew I was well prepared.

James ran beside me, in case I needed something. I appreciated having him there for so many reasons; and he played an integral part in me finishing that day. It helped to have someone to keep pace with and to strategize with, as our strides fell into step and I mirrored mine to James'. We didn't talk too much, but James and I decided I should definitely run the first eight miles, and then I could walk fast and jog the last couple miles in order to come in under the allotted time.

When overwhelming fatigue caused my legs to 'have a mind of their own,' James forced me stop and drink. When I felt overwhelmed and foggy because of the fatigue, and I seemed a bit 'off to him, he forced me to talk so I'd have to focus again.

I ran the first eight miles and then slowed down to a fast walk, like James and I had planned. There weren't many people alongside the road at this point in the run, but I saw one guy standing at the road's edge up ahead in the distance.

"Ryan?" I yelled out when we made eye contact. "Ryan Shepherd?! What are you doing here?"

"I saw on Facebook that you'd be here today; so I figured I'd come out and support you," he said as he also fell in step beside me. "I called Cindy and told her I'd be waiting for you along the route."

"You drove over an hour, just to come out here for *me?*" I asked. "Man, I haven't seen you in *15 years!* That's so incredible!"

"Of course! I wouldn't miss it!" Ryan said. "I was surprised no one stopped me when I walked out near the course, but here I am!"

I was so touched by yet another friend's support. It was amazing to me that he was out there!

"Sorry, I can't talk too much," I told him as I measured my breathing, "But we can talk at the end."

"No problem. I understand. I'll be right here beside you though."

As Ryan, James and I walked and ran, a woman came up beside me and she kept pace with us too.

"Mind if I run with you?" she asked as she focused on the route in front of us.

"Not at all."

I tried not to talk much and to preserve my energy, but she talked to me as we began to run again at Mile 11. She explained that she'd needed someone to run with so she could make it to the finish line.

"I'm doing this race to honor my baby," she explained, "The baby that I lost at five months."

"Wow. I'm really sorry," I offered, as my heart broke for her.

"Thanks."

She and I continued on, each focused and lost in our own thoughts, but each still keeping pace with the other. I realized all the race participants had their own reasons for being out there on that day. Their reasons were as varied and diverse as each of their own life stories. Even as different as the participants were, each of us still focused on the same finish line.

As we approached mile marker 12, James said he'd run ahead and tell my family and friends that I was coming. He sprinted ahead to let them know I'd be crossing the finish line soon.

Go! Go! Go! I thought as I waved him on. *Go! Go! Go!*

James ran back to me again minutes later, and was at my side, matching his steps with mine. Just before we got close to the finish line, Ryan and James veered off the course and let me run the last half-mile or so on my own.

"See ya at the finish line!" they yelled as I waved and smiled without speaking.

As I put one foot in front of the other, I thought of all I'd been through in the last couple years. So much had happened and transpired that had led up to that very moment in time. While I was about to cross the finish line, I knew that it really marked the *beginning* of the rest of my life and all the goodness that was yet to come. As I measured my breathing and kept running, I thanked God that I was still here and able to take a breath.

Suddenly, I heard the sounds of cheering and clapping and I saw a huge yellow inflatable marker in the distance. There was a sea of blue 'Team Atts' T-shirts worn by my friends and family and a bunch of homemade signs and banners. As everyone clapped and cheered, people shook cowbells and yelled for me as I got closer and closer to my goal. With my arms over my head, I ran across the finish line with six minutes to spare!

An official came over and hung a medal around my neck as my family and friends clapped, yelled and cheered. I walked a bit more, so my leg muscles wouldn't cramp, and then I went over and hugged everyone. They all thought they were celebrating me, and my feat, but it was really *I* who celebrated *them* and all they meant to me. Soaking wet from head to toe, with sweat running down my body and my heart still pumping hard, I tried to catch my breath. It felt great that I'd completed the ½ Ironman, and even with time to spare. But as I looked at all the faces around me, young and old, I knew why my heart was so full, and it had nothing to do with the last 70.3 miles.

Epilogue

After I finished the ½ Ironman in Muncie, we celebrated with family and friends; and then Keri and I decided to get a hotel room for the night and then drive home in the morning. The boys were happy to extend our family's adventure, needless to say. As we all fell asleep that night, I thanked God for getting me to where I was in life, and for giving me the five gifts that make my life worth living.

On the Monday afternoon following the ½ Ironman, I posted an update to my Facebook page as always:

Quick update…Day 1 of 63 days…training for
the Reed's Lake Tri*!!!*
~ Well, you didn't think I was going to STOP, did you? ~
Kicking Cancers A**!!!
GO!GO!GO!!!

GO!GO!GO!!! Playlist
Music that inspired the book.

1   To Be Young – Ryan Adams

2   Begin the Begin - REM

3   I'm Ready – Twin Shadows

4   Something's Wrong- Sloan

5   Seasons- Future Islands

6   Running Up that Hill – Kate Bush

7   The Way We Get By- Spoon

8   A Pain That I'm Used To- Depeche Mode

9   Everything Is Wrong - Interpol

10   Clinically Dead – Chad VanGaalen

11   Rise - Calla

12   Alive & Amplified – Mooney Suzoki

13   True Faith - New Order

14   Hands Up, Robert - Saint Motel

Listen to GO!GO!GO!
Rise, Fall, and Rise Again. https://itunes.apple.com/us/playlist/
go!go!go!-rise-fall-rise-again/idpl.07afaa55fd334c91a6256b77e0532914

D1286060

56040752R00088

Made in the USA
Lexington, KY
10 October 2016